Where Earth and Sky Meet

By

T A Blezard

First published by T A Blezard 2024

This book is sold subject to the condition that it shall not, by way of trade or otherwise, be lent, resold, hired out, or otherwise circulated without the author's prior consent in any form of binding or cover other than that in which it is published and without a similar condition, including this condition, being imposed on the subsequent purchaser.

The right of T A Blezard to be identified as the author of this work has been asserted by her in accordance with the Copyright, Designs and Patents Act 1988

Copyright © T A Blezard 2024

All characters in this publication are fictitious and any resemblance to real persons, living or dead, is purely coincidental.

ISBN: 9798876640116

Imprint: Independently published

CHAPTER ONE

The night after we buried my grandfather he walked straight into my room.

"Adie, why are you crying, boy?"

I stopped pretty sharp then, I can tell you. I just stared at him, standing there in his dark blue suit, his favourite, the same suit we had buried him in thirty-two hours earlier. I thought I was losing my mind.

"You have to be strong now, for your mother," he told me solemnly.

I clapped my hands over my ears, screwing my eyes up as tight as I could. There was a faint spicy smell in the room, lavender and cinnamon, and it tickled the back of my throat.

"Go away!"

I could hear the blood pulsing in my ears. When I finally dared open my eyes again, I was alone. He had done as I'd asked.

For weeks afterwards it was all I could think about: that the last thing my grandfather ever heard me say before he passed over was me telling him to get lost. I told no one. After all, what could I say? That I had started to hallucinate? That, all of a sudden, I could be walking down the road and someone would call out to me, even when there was no one there? Like that would do my rep much good at school. No one needs to be labelled 'different' and I was already different enough thanks to my dad. Add crazy to that and no one would want anything to do with me ever again.

Mum took me to a bereavement counsellor who explained that my grandfather was the first person I had been close to that had died, so naturally I was going to be upset. I didn't tell her about the voices. Instead I told her to shove her counselling sessions. Then Mum and I got into a huge argument about it and she slapped me across the face – the only time Mum has ever hit me. I knew as soon as she'd done it she was sorry but I was angry and wouldn't let her apologise. I wanted her to feel as bad as me, which was pretty mean because my grandfather was her dad and she must have been missing him heaps too.

That was nine months ago.

I still miss Babu (which is what I always called him) and I still hear the voices but I try and block them out as much as possible. Maybe I'm going the same way as my dad. Grandpa Cooper, my other grandfather, let it slip once that they had taken him to a shrink when he was about my age. I didn't like to ask what for. You could tell as soon as he'd said it he was wishing he hadn't. He doesn't like to admit that there could be anything wrong with his family, you see. Any problems must have come from my mum's side, because we're a different colour to him. Mum calls him 'old school'. I call him racist.

We don't see so much of the Coopers now because Mum and Dad are divorced. Besides, they live in Birmingham and me and Mum live in east London. But once a year my mother still takes me to visit. She says it's important because, whatever else they may be, they are still family.

"If *you* can't change their perceptions of the world, then who will?" she asks me, pushing me up to their frosted-glass front door, year after year.

The last time we were up there was just before Christmas. Grandma Cooper shoved a card at my mother, nodding towards me.

"There's money inside, for the boy. I don't know what to buy him. I don't know what he likes." (That's how they talk: as if I'm invisible or not sitting right there on the sofa with them.)

"You could ask him," my mother said, taking the envelope.

Grandma Cooper shook her head. "*You* get him something. You know him best."

My mother, polite as always, just smiled.

"Say thank you, Adie," she told me quietly.

I scowled. "Thank you Adie."

Mum sighed and Grandma Cooper's face twisted into an unnatural smile.

Grandpa Cooper cleared his throat awkwardly. "You know, I er, well we were both sorry to hear about your father, about Tim."

Mum flinched a little, surprised I guess that he should mention Babu. She reached for my hand, massaging it in hers. "Yes, thank you. It was a great shock."

Grandpa Cooper coughed again. "Indian man, wasn't he?"

"Yes." I could feel Mum growing uncomfortable beside me. I was ready to jump up and punch the old-school racist if I had to.

"Weak hearts," announced Grandpa Cooper authoritatively. "And eyes. Bad eyes, generally. As a race, I mean."

"He got hit by a taxi," Mum pointed out and there was a long, heavy pause.

"Maybe he didn't see it," offered Grandma Cooper. "On account of his bad eyes."

Mum tightened her grip on my hand, crushing my knuckles.

"Anyway, all I'm saying is, I heard he was a good man," conceded Grandpa Cooper, frowning as if the words tasted bad in his mouth, "a very good man."

Mum managed to smile. "He was," she replied softly. "We miss him very much, don't we, Adie?"

Given the strangeness of my family, let me tell you about my friends instead. I have lots of friends. Or maybe they're what you'd call acquaintances: people you can hang with, have a smoke with, a laugh and a joke with, talk bullshit to without really saying anything at all. But there are lots of them. Lots of likes. Lots of follows.

I suppose when I think about it, the only two people I'd class as *real-life* friends would be Cara and Paul: Cara because we talk about books and films and stuff, and Paul because of his interest in music. I get stick sometimes for being mates with them because they're not the coolest people in school but I'm certainly not about to cut them loose just to please a few loud-mouthed social-media morons.

We were hanging out now, me and Cara, waiting for the end of afternoon break.

"Dystopian."

She dropped the word like someone might drop a water bomb off a high roof. Now she was watching for my reaction.

I just stared blankly back at her. I knew exactly what it meant but wasn't about to tell her this.

"Diss what now?"

"To-pi-an," she said, clearly and slowly. "Like in The Hunger Games or Divergent, by Victoria Roth?" Cara looked at me as if I was stupid, playing right into my hands. "You know: a bleak futuristic vision, all death and destruction and robots and evil governments controlling everything you do and think...?"

"It sounds effed up," I told her. "Why would you want to read about an effed up society when we already live in an effed up society?"

She held my gaze for a while. "And why do you always play dumb all the time? You read more than I do."

"Just looking at the pictures mostly," I assured her.

The bell rang. I pushed myself off the wall of the corridor, scooping up my bag. "Come on. Don't want to be late for Mr Harry."

Cara sighed as she reluctantly lumbered after me.

I turned. "Oh, and by the way, it's Veronica: *Veronica* Roth who wrote Divergent!" and I could hear her muttering and swearing all the way outside. Slam dunk. It's all in the timing, you know.

As Cara and I crossed the quad to C Block where we had history someone hissed at me.

"Where you going, Blud?"

Curtis and his gang were slouched against the wall between the two blocks, peeking furtively round the corner. I shrugged back, like the answer should have been obvious. Then again, things are never obvious to Curtis. I could feel Cara's unease as her feet slowed alongside mine, not knowing whether to wait or go on alone.

"We got history," I told Curtis, stepping over to his little gang, glancing back over my shoulder to Cara.

He sucked air through his teeth. "What's history except a bunch of stuff not happening now?" He twisted his hand round, showing me the spliff cupped inside.

"Adie?" Cara called nervously, backing up a couple of paces.

Mason Aboko sniggered and made a loud beeping noise, like when a lorry reverses, and Cara stopped instantly. She looked at me, hurt.

I turned back to Curtis. "Maybe another time, yeah?"

He raised his eyebrows, clearly annoyed. He isn't used to people saying no to him.

"Maybe." We bumped fists and then he and his crew melted back into the shadows to go and get high before home time. I started to walk again.

"I don't know why you're friends with them," Cara muttered angrily, still smarting over the dig at her weight.

"S'funny, they say the same to me about you," I replied.

After Mr Harry had finally dried up about the far-reaching effects of the British Empire in Victorian times we were free to go home. Curtis was nowhere to be seen and I almost wished I'd said yes to him earlier. It was raining now and I didn't have a coat. Summer still felt like an eternity away.

"You want to eat round mine?" I asked Cara. "It's Thai Tuesday."

Cara frowned. "It's Wednesday today."

"Oh, well we're having Thai anyway."

She was still frowning. "I don't know if I like Thai. It's hot, right?"

"Kind of."

Cara made a face. But if she never came round mine to eat, she wouldn't know that not every meal has to come in a bucket or have supersized fries with it. Don't get me wrong, I love that stuff too, but not all the time. My mum's something of a health nut when it comes to food.

"I've got homework to do," she said so I swung my bag up onto my shoulder and turned to go. "But thanks anyway," she called. "See you tomorrow, yeah?"

But I was already stuffing my ears with a bit of Stormzy and couldn't hear if she said anything else. You can only try and help someone so much.

CHAPTER TWO

The smell of curry and spices hit me as soon as I opened the back door but that's not unusual in our house. Food is a big part of daily life in the Cooper household. From the age I could hold a knife properly, my mum had me helping in the kitchen. Mum said I had to learn where food came from, and how to prepare it. At fifteen I make a mean Babute, let me tell you, which is like a sweet curry with apricots in it. It comes from central Africa, but we eat stuff from all over the world.

Sara, my grandmother, was tending the wok and she gave the sizzling contents a quick flick with her spoon as I came in.

"Ah, the one-who-seeks-enlightenment returns," she smiled. "Perfectly timed as always."

"And I keep telling you, I won't get no enlightenment at that dumb-arse school, that's for damn sure."

She clicked her tongue. She doesn't like to hear me swear.

"Keep your mind open and enlightenment nearly always finds you," she replied.

I was about to say something else but my mother was suddenly there in the doorway.

"Mind open, mouth closed," she warned. "Go wash up for dinner."

Cara always tells me my house is not like anyone else's. 'It's like stepping into a different world,' she giggles, and whether she means the way we eat, or the pictures on the wall, or the way my family dress sometimes, I'm never really sure. My grandmother is from Uganda but she came to England in the early seventies when my grandfather got kicked out of the country. He, as you've probably realised, was Indian, and back then, a load of Asian people who lived in Uganda got chucked out by the President, Idi Amin. (You see, you don't just learn history at school.)

Years and years and years ago, for a young African girl to hook up with an Indian man was a scandal so Nana Sara and Babu kept their relationship a secret. Sara Obote was not like the other girls in her village anyway. Though her education had been cut short at the age of eleven to gather firewood and provide meals for the family, she wanted to learn about the world far beyond her village. And when she fell in love with the mysterious man who sold cloth in the neighbouring town, her life changed in ways that even *she* couldn't have imagined.

They started a secret affair, two misfits who didn't feel they belonged anywhere except together, or so she says. Nana Sara tells me the story over and over. She has a twinkle in her eyes when she starts it and a tear by the end. Until he got hit by that taxi, they hadn't spent a day apart in fifty years.

Maybe it was a mistake to come to England, she'll say when she's feeling low. But perhaps if they had stayed, Babu would have been hit by an elephant. Who knows? Maybe we all have a path to follow and, taxis or elephants, it doesn't matter. When your time's up, that's it.

"You feeling homesick again, Nana?" I shoved an oversized spoonful of Thai green curry and sticky rice into my gob and got a disapproving tut from my mother, who places great emphasis on good manners.

"Who knows? Maybe sometimes," she sighed wistfully, dabbing her watery eyes. "You should experience it for yourself some time, Adie. Ah, the smells, the colours. It's the colours mainly. Such beautiful colours." But I guess what she was really remembering was Babu.

Nana Sara still wears bright colours. She always has a scarf round her shoulders, a swathe of lemon yellow, or deep purple or emerald green against her dark skin. They remind her of Babu and his cloth shop, I suppose.

Mum was nodding by this point, her head going up and down, up and down, and that same dreamy look on her face like she was remembering it all too: the hot dusty roads, monkeys hooting in the trees, elephants tramping through the brush on a hot shimmering horizon (that's how I imagine it anyway, you know, from the wildlife programmes I've seen on TV...David Attenborough's voice droning softly in the background...).

"Come on," I scoffed. "Don't *you* start. You were born in Stepney!"

"Adie," she shook her head. "We are each of us children of the world. You of all people should know that. Why is everyone so quick to put up barriers?"

"To keep the elephants out?"

Perhaps that's why Grandpa Cooper has such a tall fence all the way round his house on Oakwood Drive. He probably never had to worry about elephants before – before my dad met my mum, I mean. Africa was just another place he would never visit. But once I was born all those distant places were brought right into his living-room and here I was: part African, part Indian, part London and part pure white

Brummy, calling him Grandpa. Maybe that's what he means as we sit on his sofa, eating pukka pie and chips off our knees in front of Coronation Street, and he says things like 'I don't know what's happening to this bleeding country'. We all just look down into our mushy peas and say nothing. Cara would probably love it, though.

CHAPTER THREE

These days I've been relegated to the box room. Mum has the main bedroom and Nana Sara has the second room. She came to live with us after Babu died. 'Too many echoes', she said, 'too many ghosts'. She sold the house where they had always lived and divided the money between my mum and her three brothers. Mum put the money in the bank, she said for when I go to college (not that Dad wouldn't cover my fees with the loose change in his back pocket) but to be honest Uni is looking less and less likely. I guess I've let a few things slide since my grandfather died.

On my desk, there's a picture of Babu, or Balbir Poria to use his given name. Balbir means full of strength but apparently when he came to England, English people found it too difficult to say, so my grandfather (not about to be deterred by the mispronunciation of his name) said 'just call me Tim: Tall Indian Man', so that's what everyone knew him as: Tim. I guess there are many different kinds of strength.

He used to tell me the most fantastic stories of what it was like to grow up in Africa, which had been the Porias' home ever since his great, great grandfather was brought over from India at the end of the eighteen-nineties to help build the Uganda Railway. He told me stories about that too, even though it was long before he was born; told me how thousands of the slave labour force on the railway died in the most terrible conditions, but I guess my great, great, great grandfather was one of the lucky ones, the strong ones: he survived, settling there for generations to come.

Babu showed me rare photographs from his childhood: him and his sister posing at the equator sign on the Kampala Masaka Road, marking the line at which the two hemispheres – North and South – come together; another one of him leaning over the Owen Falls Dam, barely tall enough to peep over the parapet; and then later, as a grown-up, a photo of his cloth shop downtown, a small dark hole in the wall crammed with long rolls of fabric. The pictures were in black and white so I could only imagine the colours. He kept the photographs, rare and precious as they were, in a rusty biscuit tin and every time I visited, I would beg him to show them to me again, even though each one had long since been imprinted on my memory's hard-drive. Photos are like that. Look at them for long enough and you'd swear you were actually there. Tell a story over and over and you'd believe you had lived it yourself.

Above the picture of my grandfather, there are also a couple of my dad. Most of the photos come from magazine articles and clippings, haphazardly pasted together in a kind of collage. I used to collect them a lot when I was younger, when he and Mum were still together, but after a while it seemed like more and more of the articles were saying bad things so I stopped. Nowadays he still crops up in places like Kerrang! and Q Magazine – he was the front man in a rock band when I was little – but mostly they're just surprised he's still alive.

Of course they've been planning a comeback for as long as I can remember. Oh yes. They're always talking about going back into the studio or organising another major tour, "gigging like the old days" says Dad with that foggy look in his eyes. I've heard it a million times. But they don't have the hunger anymore; don't have the financial incentive they did in the early days when he and my mum had just met and were still broke, before Voodoo Mary made it to the big time, many moons ago.

Now you understand why I can get away with saying 'no' to the likes of Curtis Laycock. We met each other at the age of seven, both of us enrolled in this Saturday school for would-be child actors (back when we were both young enough for our parents to believe anything was possible, I guess). When we were eight, Dad took us in a limo for a night-ride through the city of London. Me and Curtis stood on the back seat with our heads just poking out of the roof – like Babu peeking over the wall of the dam – screaming at the tops of our lungs like a couple of demented loonies. It was sick. We had McDonald's at midnight while Dad drank vodka neat out of the bottle and Curtis still talks about it. Totally sick.

Neither me nor Curtis go to stage school anymore and would probably never have seen each other after the age of nine, when we gave up acting and make-believe. But Mum and me moved house after the divorce and, surprise surprise, suddenly Curtis and I were in the same high school. Not that we hang out so much. He's got his friends like Mason Aboko and I've got, well Cara, I guess, and Paul Timmins (who plays violin in the school orchestra). Damn. When did I get so uncool?

I put the picture of Dad back on the bookshelf and reached for another one of Babu, examining the familiar photograph in its shiny silver surround: him and Nana Sara outside their old shop in Brick Lane.

"You still up?" Mum poked her head round the door, then edged in as I put down the silver frame.

"Yeah, you know, just thinking about stuff."

"Mind open," she nodded. "That's always good."

"Is Nana Sara all right?"

She squinted at me. "Sure. Why?"

"Well, you know, getting a bit teary over dinner and everything."

Mum sat on my bed. "It's hard, Adie." She reached for the picture of Babu with a sigh. "It's all still very raw."

"Yeah, I know. Sorry." I felt shitty for making her feel sad again.

Everyone still misses him: all my aunts and uncles and cousins, friends and neighbours. Enigmatic, that's what he was, and you couldn't help but like him (even those who couldn't pronounce his name).

Mum smiled at me. "That's okay. Don't ever feel like you can't talk about things." She put back the photo. "He was a great man. So long as we don't forget him, then he's not truly gone."

"You know I saw him," I blurted out suddenly, "the day after the funeral. I saw him in my bedroom."

Mum just smiled a sad smile and stroked the side of my face. I wanted to tell her about the voices, about telling Babu to go away, but I was scared that she would take me to a psychiatrist; that they would say I was mad, or a liar. Mum glanced at the rest of the pictures: Dad in a shiny tux on a red carpet; him, Mum and me in LA.

"Hey Mum, what d'you think happens to people when they die?"

I saw her shoulders tense up as she turned back to me. "I don't know, Adie. Maybe you go to a better place, a better place than this. Who knows?"

She kissed me on the cheek and stood up, leaving me to insert the small white earbuds into my ears once more, allowing Motorhead's classic Ace of Spades to lull me to sleep and some other, better place, or at least one with fewer questions.

CHAPTER FOUR

Thursdays always started with PE but today I just couldn't face it so I cut school between registration and the boys' changing rooms and found myself out on Latchmere Road in my school uniform at quarter past nine in the morning. Today the sun was out and it seemed to shine just on me, spotlighting the fact that I was playing truant. I headed for the busiest streets, trying to lose myself in the early morning crowds while I figured out what to do with my unscheduled free time. I had the eerie sense of someone watching me. I guess that's what you get for having a guilty conscience: Edgar Allen Poe's Tell Tale Heart, as Cara would say.

The flow of people had soon picked me up and carried me down Riverside Way, towards the large covered market and the best Afro-Caribbean barber's this side of the river. It's where people go and hang out all day and talk about music and life and anything but haircuts, but I didn't want to go there for fear of being spotted through the big plate glass window that looks out onto the high street. Instead, I ducked through the fish market and onto the next street, thinking I might head for the little music shop on Clapton Road. Still I had the uneasy feeling of being watched.

Rounding the next corner, I stopped abruptly. An open-topped mini bus pulled by two chestnut horses stood in the middle of the road. Lying on the ground, at the back of this strange looking vehicle, was a man spread-eagled in the dirt, blood pooling out from beneath his torn clothes. One foot was caught on the bottom rung of the steps, which led up to the top deck, as if he may have slipped and become entangled on his way down. People were now crying and shouting, craned over from the upper deck, staring in horror at the bloody man just lying there below. The driver, alerted by his passengers' screams, had brought the horses to a halt and was now clambering down from his high seat at the front of the bus. The bloody man's wide glassy eyes stared straight into mine.

"What's happened to me?" I heard his voice in my head even though his lips never moved.

It was as if I had walked onto the film set of some historical drama and I glanced around expecting the director to angrily yell 'cut' at any moment. My legs started to vibrate beneath me and I'm pretty sure it was nothing to do with the rumbling of a passing tube train a hundred feet below. The carriage driver knelt down and spoke to the man. It looked very realistic.

"Yo, Cooper, where you headed?"

I spun round in a panic to find Curtis Laycock and Mason Aboko trailing after me. For a moment I couldn't work out what they were doing here. Were they extras in the film? Curtis certainly wasn't in his school uniform. Clearly whatever else he might have been doing, going to school wasn't it. I glanced back over my shoulder but the man and the open-topped bus were nowhere to be seen. Curtis stood in front of me with a strange look on his face.

"What's the matter with you, Blud?"

"Huh?" I checked over my shoulder but it was just an ordinary street, full of people doing their shopping. My heart thumped wildly beneath my school shirt. "I was bunking off," I told Curtis. Beads of sweat broke out on my top lip. I didn't want him to know I was going crazy. "You know, it's Mayhew, innit?" I said, like that explained everything.

Curtis grinned. "Yeah, I know what you mean, bruv." And he came out with a few choice expressions of his own to describe our less than inspiring PE teacher.

As I looked over my shoulder one last time, I caught Curtis and Mason exchanging glances with one another, staring after me to see what it was that I kept looking for.

"Hey, I got a bit of gear left over from yesterday if you want to kill some time," Curtis offered.

Now don't get me wrong, I know the effects drugs can have on a person. You only have to look at my father to see that. His hands shake like an old dude. But I'm not stupid either and you can only say no to Curtis Laycock so many times. Besides, I figured I needed something to stop my head from exploding.

"Sure, sounds good," I nodded.

"Yeah?" Curtis looked almost surprised and instantly I felt as though I had made a mistake.

So that's how I got wasted Thursday morning up in my bedroom with Curtis Laycock and Mason Aboko instead of running laps in PE.

My mother works during the day until three, and Thursday mornings my grandmother visits her church group, so I figured we'd have a good couple of hours undisturbed. Curtis looked round my small bedroom, clearly disappointed. Dad bought this house when he and Mum split up, as part of the divorce settlement. I'm sure she could have had something much grander if she'd pushed for it, but that's not Mum's style. Besides, at the time it was close to Babu and Nana Sara, and it was just the two of us anyway so it suited us fine, Mum said.

Mason was sparking up, hunched over on my bed. I was glad Mum had put my pyjamas in the wash so that they didn't get to see them. Not that they have pictures of trains or anything on them, mind, but you know, they're just not that cool either. I'm not exactly sure what would constitute a cool pair of PJs come to think of it (but I guess that's a dilemma for another time). Curtis picked up the picture of Babu from my desk.

"Who's this?" he demanded. "He looks like a bleedin' Paki."

I snatched it away from him. "He's dead so watch your mouth, man."

Curtis turned, a sneer curling at his lips but Mason was concentrating on the joint and wasn't there to back him up. He faced me.

"No that's cool, fam, that's cool." He picked up a photo of my dad. "Aah, here he is, the man himself. Hey, Mace, you seen this? His old man is the business, I'm telling you bro, the biz-i-ness!"

Mason looked up, taking a long deep draw. "Yeah?" He didn't seem overly interested. "What's he do then?"

Curtis swore. "I told you loads of times what he do." He swore again but Mason clearly couldn't have cared less. "He's a rock star, man. A for-real mega star. Here, put some of his music on for him, bruv."

A moment later a grungy guitar riff was booming out of my speakers along with a crunching, crashing drum beat. Curtis nodded along with it, admiring, though I'm not sure it's the kind of music he'd ever listen to if he didn't know me or my dad. Me,

I listen to anything: metal to rap, pop through to classical and everything in between.

"How come you ain't rich then?" Mason looked accusingly at me with bloodshot eyes.

I just shrugged. "What can I tell you? He blew it all on cocaine and prostitutes."

Mason passed the spliff over to Curtis. "Cool," he said to me, smiling and nodding. "That's cool."

Yeah. Cool. Like my pyjamas. I wondered if Mason knew that Curtis used to go to stage school.

I woke up a little before midday. Curtis and Mason had gone. And so had my Assassin's Creed 4 along with three pound coins that I'd emptied out of my pocket shortly before I lay down. I wondered what they'd loaded the jay with and slumped back down, feeling disorientated and heavy-headed. Downstairs someone was moving around, opening cupboards in the kitchen and I cursed, quietly, knowing that I would have to sneak out of the house to make it back before afternoon registration.

I crept downstairs, being careful to jump over the creaky step second to the bottom, then started to pad towards the front door.

"Not so fast, Adie."

Nana Sara was standing in the kitchen doorway. She may be old but there's nothing wrong with her hearing.

"I'm gonna be late."

"You didn't look so concerned about that five minutes ago."

She went back into the kitchen and I paused for a moment, debating just bolting for the door.

"You are a smart young man with the whole world in front of you just ripe for the picking," she told me, "yet you persist in throwing away the gifts that are all around you."

"I swear I don't know what you're talking about, Nana. I just fell asleep."

"Up there smoking your ganja, your hashish, whatever it is that you call it these days," she snapped back.

"Nana, some friends came over. Maybe they had some but..."

Nana Sara was there again in the doorway, fixing me with a cold, fish-eyed stare.

"You are lost Adie, like your father. And if you stay lost for too long, you will never find your way home."

"What? Like Dad, you mean?" My face had hardened, I could feel it, like I was wearing a mask that was just a little too tight.

"Your father is a good man, I know that," she conceded with a sigh. "But you need to work hard, Adie, apply yourself before it is too late. Aah, when I think of how hard your grandfather had to work to get to where he was..."

But that was a low blow, mentioning Babu like that. I grabbed at the latch.

"Save it. I'm going to school."

"You're going nowhere, Adie, running, running always running but going nowhere," she called after me but I had slammed the front door by this time.

I was halfway down the road before I wondered whether she was going to tell my mum.

CHAPTER FIVE

The home phone rang at one o'clock in the morning. I bolted upright in bed, dragged from a dream about Babu. I could hear Mum stumbling along the hallway and down the stairs while the landline continued its shrill alarm. My heart was beating in double time. Nothing good ever comes from a phone call at one in the morning on a number that only a handful of people possess.

I emerged from the box room at the same time as Nana Sara appeared bleary-eyed across the hallway from me. We both listened to Mum downstairs.

"Craig? What's happened? What's wrong? Are you kidding? What are you calling me for? Craig! Listen, I…yes, okay, calm down…You know I don't have a car. I have Adie here and my mother, what do you expect me to do? Okay, okay, I'll call John Parker for you, I'm sure I've still got his number here somewhere…" We could hear Mum moving around the living room as she listened to my father on the other end of the line. Every so often she would mumble 'uh-huh, okay, yup, uh-huh' and then there was a long sigh. "Okay Craig. You go and sleep it off. I'll see what I can do this end. Yeah, whatever. Me too."

Nana Sara and I locked eyes. Her expression was sad, resigned. She motioned with her head for me to return to bed and I slipped back inside, clicking shut the door. He was obviously drunk, my father. And in trouble too: John Parker is his solicitor. It didn't take a genius to realise he had got himself banged up in a cell again.

Mostly I was angry: angry with him for doing this to us one more time and angry with myself because more than anything I was relieved. The first thing you think when the phone goes at one in the morning is that this time he's done it: choked on his own vomit, crashed his car off a bridge, and that this is the call to tell you he's finally run out of free rides. And I was so angry at myself for feeling relieved because sometimes I just wish he'd hurry up and finish it. Get it over with so we can all move on with our lives.

It was too late to make Saturday's papers but the tabloids had all picked it up in time for Sunday's print-run. And it was slowly gathering momentum on social media too, I noticed. Thankfully, enough time had passed since he and Mum were together that we no longer had the press hammering on our front door for sound-bites. Mum spread the Sunday Mirror out over the breakfast table, a look of distaste pulling at her face.

"Let me see." I reached for it.

"Adie, it's just the same old, same old. I don't even know why I bought it."

I pulled the paper across the table and she sighed heavily.

"They might as well lock the man up 'cos he sure ain't free now, for all the money he got," murmured Nana Sara, shaking her head. "He's shackled to them demons like he in chains." I caught her eye. "You see, Adie, no good ever comes of these poisons you want to put in yourself."

Mum snorted. "Over my dead body is Adie getting involved in drink and drugs, Mama."

I looked back down at the newsprint still unsure of why my grandmother had not said anything to her about last Thursday.

Craig Cooper, former front man of 90s Brit rock legends Voodoo Mary, was arrested Friday night after a brawl in a night-club escalated and ended in a high speed limo-chase through the streets of north London. Cooper, 47, who has previously been treated for drug and alcohol addictions, admitted assaulting his chauffeur, 56-year-old Derek Shepherd, before taking the limo on a twenty-minute tear-up through city streets, endangering lives and causing several thousand pounds worth of damage before police were finally able to bring the vehicle to a stop.

There was no need to read further. I pushed the paper back into the centre of the table as Mum and Nana Sara waited for my reaction.

"Like you said – same old, same old." I scraped my chair back.

"Don't you want to talk about it?" asked Mum.

But everything had already been said.

I sat in front of the TV, punching through the channels. At one point Dad's face was there in front of me and I quickly changed over. I watched some cartoons and Mum brought me through a sandwich for lunch. I remained there all afternoon with the TV on, curtains drawn. Mum and Nana Sara stayed in the kitchen talking in low whispers. Finally, the smells of dinner wafted through to me, at which point I got up and went out.

I suppose what I should have done was go to Cara's. She always listens when I've got something to offload. Or I could have dropped round at Paul's and mucked about on his computer for a couple of hours. He has an electronic keyboard that he lets me bang out a few chords on (I can't really play that much but once he feeds it through his software it actually sounds all right). Any of that might have been fun on a usual Sunday night except this wasn't a usual Sunday night anymore. I just wanted to forget all about my dad and the only way I knew how to do that was to get drunk, or high, or both.

    I headed over to the little park at the end of Bishop's Road where I knew Curtis and his crew usually hung out but it was empty so I looped slowly round the block, wondering how I could get hold of some booze. There was a Tesco Express on the corner of Victoria Road and Totterdown Street and it sold alcohol but I suspected I had zero chance of buying anything without I.D. or looking about twenty-five (which I don't). And I didn't have the guts to try and swipe something, so I was stuffed.

    I skulked up Totterdown Street making my way back towards Bishop's Park again, wondering how it was that when you actually wanted to bump into someone, they were nowhere to be found. Perching myself on the back of a bench, I stared at the swings and the slide, all forlorn-looking without kids playing on them. But it had been raining earlier and they were still glistening with water. Besides, most children would be having their evening meals now, a thought which reminded me of my own hunger, making me all the more depressed. I pulled out my phone to text Cara.

    There was a movement at the far end of the park and I looked up. The Curtis Laycock crew were ambling across the grass, all swaying and swaggering, aware that I was here – in their park – and watching them. Funny, but at that split second, I almost wished they hadn't turned up as if I knew that this was the point where things could only get worse. Had I just sloped home five minutes earlier, Mum would have been there to make it all better, a hot bowl of food, Nana Sara, TV, my bed, my Xbox. Suddenly I really wanted *not* to be here in Bishop's Park with Curtis and his merry band bouncing towards me – even though that was exactly what I'd been wishing for just moments before.

"Adie, my man," Curtis drawled on his approach. "Wagwaan?"

We bumped fists. Mason was there and PeeWee – his two shadows – along with an older guy that I didn't know, who Curtis introduced as Jay. He grunted at me and that was that, all I needed to know about him.

"So what draws you up here, eh?" Curtis asked. "Don't usually see you out this late."

I was about to point out that it wasn't late when I realised he was having a dig so I let it slide.

"Oh you know, just hanging."

Curtis raised his eyebrows at me like he knew there was more to it. Maybe he had seen the papers. I wondered whether I should say something about my dad before one of them did. PeeWee sparked up a spliff and the moment got lost in the smoke. They made themselves comfortable on the bench beside me, Jay pulling out two bottles of WKD from inside his jacket and cracking them both open. I watched as they got passed along the line. Curtis took a couple of mouthfuls and then paused, as if he were considering skipping over me. I waited to see if he was going to make me pay for all the times I'd said 'no' to him before. He finally handed me the bottle but as I grabbed for it he whisked it out of reach. He sniggered, then held it out again, and on the third time I was able to take a big long gulp hoping it would do the trick.

"You want to be careful hanging round here," Curtis warned me as he sucked in on the spliff. "Lotta bad people hang round here, Adie, my man, lotta bad people."

"What? Like you, you mean?"

Curtis looked at me just long enough for my heart to miss a beat before he laughed and I was able to breathe again. The rest of them smiled too at that point but I knew I was on shaky ground. Curtis had always cut me way more slack than he did for anybody else, but that had to stop one of these days – when he realised there would be no more limo rides.

"I know you joking with me, Blud, and that's cool. I don't mind it when people joke with me, when *friends* joke with me, right? You get me?"

I smiled but it took all the effort I could muster for the muscles in my face to work like that. I stared down at my high tops on the wooden slats of the bench, pretended to pick something off the knee of my jeans, aware that Curtis was watching me the whole time.

"Me and Adie go way back," he announced presently to the rest of the gang.

I kept looking down. 'Here it comes,' I thought and sure enough he was telling them about that time in the back of the limo when we were eight. Talk about same old, same old.

"...blew it all on coke and prostitutes," Mason finished off, as if he had known my dad back then too, another clown in the circus that was my life.

PeeWee whistled through his teeth.

"Sweet," grunted Jay.

"But you's just the same as everyone else here, Adie," Curtis told me seriously. "PeeWee's dad is doing ten for armed robbery, ain't that right, PeeWee? I got nine half brothers and sisters thanks to my father and only time any of us see him is when he want something. And Mace here, well he don't even know who his old man is, do you Mace? Could be *your* old man for all he knows."

Mason Aboko growled back, like maybe this was something he didn't want to share with the world and its dog.

"I'm just saying," Curtis said, in a level, no-messing kind of way. "Adie here ain't no Mr Big-Shot-Thinks-He's-Better-Than-Everyone-Else. He's just somebody else with a deadbeat dad, same as you or PeeWee or whoever. Ain't that right, Adie?"

So he had seen the news after all. Suddenly they were all looking at me again.

"I guess." My shoulders twitched awkwardly through my hoody.

"See? He guesses." Curtis laughed, then lunged towards me, grinning, and half-punched half-pushed me backwards off the seat. I tumbled into the bushes behind and they all guffawed with laughter.

For a moment I couldn't work out what I was doing on my back in the grass. It occurred to me this could very easily go one of two ways. I cursed but kept it light so as not to antagonise them any further and I got to my feet, brushing myself off. "Shit, I need a drink."

Curtis looked at me for just a second too long, then burst out laughing again and helped me clamber back up onto the bench, thumping me across the shoulders.

"Get my man here a drink," he ordered but by now both bottles were empty. "What are you guys playing at?" Curtis sounded annoyed. "This man here is used to the fine things in life, ain't that right, Adie? The *fine* things."

"Yeah, I could use some sherbet myself right now," sniffed Jay excavating his nose with one finger. "Ain't nothing finer than that."

"I'm sorry about this." Curtis turned to me, dripping mock-sincerity while there was a mutual scraping about for change amongst the others and I wished he wouldn't keep singling me out like this. I guess he no more knew how to be friends with me than I did with him. "Come on." He nodded his head towards the park gate. "We're going to get you that drink." And before I knew it we were all heading out of the park, I guessed to the Tesco's Express to re-fuel, Curtis once more treating me like visiting royalty.

Jay came out of the mini-market a little while later brandishing a two-litre brown plastic bottle of cider, some cigarettes and a packet of sausage rolls. We ripped into everything as we walked, the sweet alcohol on an empty stomach making me feel sick, just one cold sausage roll to mop it up. We turned into another road. I thought they would be heading back to the park, but at that point fate intervened for the second time that night.

Halfway up the road is The China Dragon restaurant and takeaway, and as usual cars were parked all along the street as the drivers went in for their spring rolls and pork balls. My stomach rumbled at the idea.

"I love Chinese food!" sighed Curtis as we neared the Dragon and I wondered whether this was my cue to buy them all dinner – because, of course, Curtis would assume I was loaded on account of my deadbeat father.

A car raced past us and came to a screeching halt a little further up, hazard lights blinking, double-parking level with the Dragon's doors. My mum always says God gave us legs so that we can walk and if he'd wanted us to drive everywhere he'd have given us wheels instead of feet. Why she popped into my head at that exact moment I have no idea. A blast of music pierced the still evening as the driver opened the door and bounded into the restaurant. We ambled up to the car, which had just been left, orange lights flashing, stereo on, engine rumbling, in the middle of the road. I turned to look through the large windows of the Chinese to see the man being handed a plastic bag full of takeaway containers, just as Curtis reached his hand out to the driver's door handle.

"Get in," he barked and next thing I knew we were all piling inside the guy's car.

Before we could even get the doors closed Curtis had released the handbrake, shoved it into gear and roared off up the road.

I was in the back seat and was very nearly thrown out as we rounded the far corner. I only just managed to heave shut the door as Mason twisted round beside me, pushing me out of the way so he could stare meanly out the back window, the guy with the plastic bag of takeaway food disappearing from view, mouthing inaudible threats and exclamations of disbelief.

"Well, what he expect, man leave keys in like that?" Curtis shouted round to us, almost clipping a parked car as he did so.

Jay was in the front seat next to him, giving him what sounded like driving tips, while the other two were giggling and cursing like they couldn't quite believe it either.

"Is this always how you spend your Sundays?" I managed to ask Curtis.

I tried not to sound impressed. Or scared.

"Sure, why not?" He turned to me and then Jay had to grab the wheel and push it back the other way so that we didn't mount the pavement and Curtis got mad and batted his hand off it.

He crunched the gearbox before shooting through a red light.

"The feds are going to notice you keep driving like that!" Mason warned him and at that point Curtis slammed on the brakes and Mason went flying between the two front seats.

"You want to drive?" Curtis snarled as Mason untangled himself and sat back down in the middle of the backseat, instantly shoving me up against the side again, as if it had somehow been my fault.

"Come on, let's get out of here," snapped Jay as someone beeped impatiently from behind.

There was more angry shunting of gears and then we were off, the old streets of home falling away in a sickening blur.

PeeWee was rolling a joint in his lap, shouting at Curtis to take it steady, and Jay was glugging on the cider again. He passed it into the back seat, Mason grabbing hold of it before I could reach it.

"Hurry up with that smoke, man," Curtis instructed PeeWee, irritably. "Let's box out this whip!"

I took a couple of mouthfuls of cider. The alcohol and adrenaline were both pumping fast now and I felt wired and spaced out as if I wasn't really there. Moments later the sweet smell of skunk was filling the little car while Jay raided the glove box for anything worth taking. He found a pair of ladies' knickers and tossed them gleefully into the back seat, laughing and cursing. I found myself wondering what the guy with the panties in the glove box had ordered from The China Dragon, wishing we'd robbed his takeaway rather than his motor.

The air in the backseat grew thick and hot as I watched the streets of east London disappearing away from us at increasing speed. Curtis took the flyover which deposited us on a different side of town and we drove around with the stereo pounding out its beats and everyone agreed that Panty Man, as he had now become, had good taste in tunes if nothing else. Then Curtis spotted an empty retail park, the shops all closed this late on a Sunday and he turned into it and spent the next five minutes throwing the car round while he performed handbrake turns for us.

Finally he stopped and we shared the rest of the cider and PeeWee rolled another joint. Jay got out the car and went for a slash. Then everyone else had to go too.

"Won't there be cameras?" PeeWee asked as he piled back inside, slamming the door with unnecessary force.

"Your dick camera-shy?" smirked Curtis but then he realised what PeeWee was getting at and we all peered furtively out of the windows.

"Can't see none," said Jay.

"There's always cameras," warned Mason, sliding down lower in the backseat.

"Shut up about the damn cameras," Curtis barked. "Think where we're gonna go."

"Let's just bounce, man," urged Mason.

"Let's go to Brighton," suggested PeeWee but this was instantly shot down by Curtis who asked why the hell anyone would want to go to Brighton.

"The sea?" replied PeeWee.

I wondered what was so wrong with Brighton. I wondered if Curtis had even seen the sea for real before.

"We ain't going to Brighton," Curtis snapped back, cursing quietly as he manhandled the gearbox again getting ready for our departure, revving but not moving.

"Well, where *are* we going?" demanded Jay and you could tell Curtis was getting flustered because clearly he had no idea and was only now realising that doing handbrake turns in a retail park in a stolen car was probably not the wisest decision he had made all day.

PeeWee wound down his window and tossed out the empty cider bottle. Jay twisted round in his seat.

"Hey, there'll be fingerprints on that. Pick it back up."

PeeWee faltered, unsure, but when Jay kept staring at him he got out of the car, swearing under his breath. As soon as his feet hit the tarmac Curtis stamped on the accelerator.

"Ras klaat!" sniggered Jay.

PeeWee only just managed to jump out of the way as we tore off. Jay and Mason boomed with laughter. PeeWee stood there hollering and waving his arms, stamping his feet and quickly pulling up the hood on his sweatshirt against any hidden cameras. Curtis slammed on the brakes and swung round, heading straight for PeeWee, who turned and started to run as Curtis floored the accelerator, yanking the wheel at the very last minute just as PeeWee took a spectacular dive like a goalie lunging for the ball. Me and Mason were flung sideways. I cracked my head hard on the window before we were both thrown back the other way. Curtis slowed and came round again, this time at a crawl and we could hear the swearing from PeeWee as he tentatively reached for the door handle. Of course as soon as he lifted his leg Curtis was off again and PeeWee fell back onto the hard concrete. In the distance came the faint whine of a police siren and my blood chilled at the sound. Curtis heard it too. He swung back round.

"Get in," he hollered.

"Not if you're gonna…" started PeeWee.

"Just get in!" shouted Curtis. "Can't you hear that?"

PeeWee leapt into the back seat beside Mason and me, then Curtis was off again, turning the car into a plane as we were briefly airborne on the ramp out of the car park. It occurred to me then that we could all be killed out here tonight, and I wished I could be anywhere else other than the backseat of a stolen car with Curtis Laycock behind the wheel.

CHAPTER SIX

The mood in the car had quickly gone from just pissing around to deadly serious. Curtis was leaning forward against the wheel, as if getting that bit closer to the windscreen would aid his concentration, and all the other cars were coming up on us at alarming speed. I tightened my grip around the back of Jay's seat, my arms locked straight, bracing myself for the inevitable impact. Despite the very real possibility of death, not a one of us was going to be soft enough to put on our seat belts.

In the wing mirror, I glimpsed a flash of blue lights, some distance behind, weaving in and out of the cars. My senses seemed to have collapsed in on themselves as dusk started to fall and the only things that stood out were the sudden green glow from the dash, streaks of white light from oncoming cars, horns wailing and dying as other vehicles were forced to take evasive action to Curtis' erratic driving, and that ever present flash of a following police car.

Curtis took the next roundabout the wrong way and threw the car into the road on the right, gaining a little distance from the cop car in the process.

"You're losing them," Jay announced triumphantly as I glanced forward and saw the needle on the speedo creep up again from forty to fifty to sixty.

We were in a residential area now and it seemed like the police were holding back a little. I almost allowed myself to believe that this could actually end okay and we'd all get out unscathed.

Curtis continued to press on the accelerator and the car hit seventy as it approached a zebra crossing with people on it. I saw them look up, then scream as they realised we weren't stopping and scatter like the splatter of paintball then, just as quickly, they were behind us, arms flailing, frantic voices raised but dying almost instantly, and we were still going. I looked in the mirror. The police car was behind us too but it was definitely dropping back.

"Pussies," smirked Curtis as he noticed the distance between us opening up.

But moments later we all saw the lights of a second police car turning into the bottom of the road ahead, cutting off our escape, and I realised this was far from over. Curtis yanked the wheel again and I swear I felt the whole thing tip onto its side before we were speeding through another narrow road at close to sixty miles an hour. There was a crunch of metal as something underneath the car sheared off and we took to the air once more over a speed hump, then smacked down hard. We all grunted as the wheels made contact with the ground, teeth slamming together.

I looked up. Looming ahead of us in the car's headlights were two white concrete bollards. I guess if anyone had stopped to read the road signs, we might have seen that this was a dead-end but at the time no one did. Curtis stomped desperately on the brakes but it was the bollards that actually stopped us and next thing I knew I was tumbling over the front seat, on top of someone, all of us in a battered, stupefied daze. Before I could make sense of what was happening, I was being dragged roughly out of the vehicle. I thought it was the cops but in the next breath we were running blindly down an alley and through a labyrinth of dark passageways, my body doing things that my brain hadn't time to give permission for, hadn't even registered. I was aware of another set of lungs panting beside my own but I couldn't look across to see who it was. We were just running, running anywhere we could as fast as we could, like rats in a maze.

After a while we both slowed and doubled over to catch our breath. I managed to lift my head, discovering it was Jay, Jay who was bent double beside me. We straightened up, trying to stop our panting and control our breathing long enough that we could listen and work out where the cops were.

"I think we lost 'em," Jay hissed, gulping down great lungfuls of air between each sentence. "But we gotta keep moving." And suddenly I was running again, even though my legs burned with the effort and my chest felt like I was wearing a t-shirt made of lead. But Jay had hold of me and I had no choice in the matter.

We took another couple of alleyways and found ourselves in a dead-end, an eight-foot wall, blocking our exit. Against it were some communal waste bins and Jay clambered on top of them so I did the same. Next moment he had launched himself blindly over the back wall of the estate and without thinking I followed. The drop on the other side was way longer than either of us had anticipated and we both hit the ground hard. I bit back a yelp of pain, my ankle twisting over as the ground slammed into both knees. Jay was already standing up, brushing himself off like he did this kind of thing all the time.

"Just act normal and we'll be sweet."

He set off walking again and I knew that if I didn't hobble after him he was going to leave me right where I was. I bit down hard on my bottom lip to stop from crying out in agony with each excruciating step and somehow managed to limp after him.

We were round the back of a row of garages and at first I thought he was looking for another car to steal to take us back home. After a while I realised he was just scanning the area, getting his bearings. He pushed me to the top of the road as my pace started to drag again.

"Stop walking like a dick. You want people to see you?" He flipped up his hood and headed off down a well-lit high street somewhere in a part of London I didn't know.

"Where are we?" I don't know why I thought he'd have the answer.

"Keep going." He coughed and spat onto the pavement.

I ran another couple of painful steps to draw level with him and then adopted a kind of skipping-walk as a way of keeping my weight off my left ankle as much as possible.

I felt very vulnerable on this unfamiliar street, like I had been dropped from a spaceship into an alien land and any moment now the inhabitants were going to come out and capture us. And if that didn't happen then a cop car was almost certainly going to pull us over. I tried to imagine what my mother would say about that. I could see the look on Nana Sara's face. At one point a police car *did* go past and I felt my legs become stiff and unwieldy but I was careful not to break stride with Jay and we just mooched on, hands in our pockets, super-casual, heads down, hoods up, as the police car cruised slowly along the road ahead of us.

"You got any funds left?" Jay asked and I pulled a couple of pound coins out of my jeans pocket to show him.

He snatched them off me. "You got an oyster, something that can get us back home?"

I shook my head, imagining Cara at that moment in a pair of sparkly red shoes clicking her heels together and going 'there's no place like home, there's no place like home, there's...' Jay suddenly yanked me into a kebab shop and the meaty smell made the saliva in my mouth leak out. Behind us the police car had doubled back and was now crawling up the high street towards us. We watched it in the mirror on the shop wall. I started to read the food options on the big plastic menu boards behind the counter: doner (chicken or lamb or both), kofte, kofte and doner, kofte and shish, shish with chips, kofte and doner with chips... When the cop car had gone Jay pushed me back out through the door and I realised we weren't getting a kebab after all.

"Come on," he grunted, clearly irritated with my slow pace, then suddenly darted across the road through a gap in the traffic, leaving me standing on the pavement opposite.

I had to wait for a transit van before I could cross and I looked up to see where he'd disappeared to. There, halfway down the next road, was a tube station. I felt my heart lift, never having been so pleased to see the London underground network before.

"Where d'you think Curtis is?" I panted.

"How should I know? I'm not his bleedin' mother."

We walked into the deserted station. There was no guarantee that the trains would even be running this late on a Sunday night and, as I realised that, I felt a plummeting of all hope for ever getting home again.

"Come on!" Jay sprinted off and I looked tiredly up just in time to see the next southbound train was due in one minute.

This late, the barriers were unmanned and open so Jay had no need of the two quid of mine in his trouser pocket and I wondered how to go about getting it back without my head being punched in. A rush of warm air blasted out of the tunnel and moments later the train was rocketing out of the blackness in a blaze of yellow light. Jay took a fistful of my sweatshirt and tugged me aboard one of the almost empty carriages. We sat down right in the middle of a row of seats, opposite one another, being careful for our feet not to touch. The doors slid shut and before long we were moving again, the familiar rocking of the carriage instantly making me want to sleep. Jay pulled out his phone and texted something before realising there was no signal down here and he cursed and stuffed it back in the pocket of his jeans, next to my two quid. I carefully stretched out my aching legs and closed my eyes just so I wouldn't have to see him anymore but I could hear him chuckling to himself and a part of me really wanted to punch him in the head but I couldn't raise the energy. Also I didn't have a death-wish.

The closest station to home on this line was a good one-mile walk from my house and by the time we reached our stop, I barely had the energy to stand up let alone put one foot in front of the other. Jay pushed me onto the escalator and off again at the top, then shoved me through the open barriers at the front. Outside it was drizzling and I shivered – cold, tired and hurting. We had just started to walk down the hill when Jay rounded on me and pinned me up against the tube station wall, his hand tight around my neck cutting into my windpipe.

"You say anything about tonight to anyone and you are a dead man," he breathed into my face. "You got that?"

I made a squeak, which was all the noise I could make with his hand wrapped round my throat, and he glared at me as if waiting for a reply. I stared helplessly back at him hoping to telepathically communicate my consent. He finally loosened his grip and I spluttered and coughed and held my hands protectively round my neck as I watched him slope off, backwards, looking at me and shaking his head. I stayed where I was against the rough wall. Clearly he was done with my company.

When I could no longer see him I set off too, very slowly, in the general direction of home. Even though it was early June, I don't think I have ever felt as cold or as miserable as I did that night and with every step I became more cold and more miserable, the tiredness wringing out every last drop of energy from my battered body. I couldn't even lift my head to check as I stepped blindly off the kerb, hurling myself back with fright as an oncoming car blared its angry horn at me.

I was limping badly by this time and bursting for a slash again so I took a pee in an alleyway and nearly gagged on the smell of my own urine then hobbled back into the light and headed home, one agonizing step at a time. Just between you and me, I felt like crying.

CHAPTER SEVEN

The drizzle had become rain as I slid my key ever so gently into the lock. My sweatshirt and jeans clung to my body as though I had just taken a swim fully-clothed, and all I could think about was getting warm. I closed the front door as softly as possible, trying not to make any sound but, as I turned around, someone flicked on the hall light to reveal Mum and Nana Sara standing there in the lounge doorway staring back at me. We all blinked a couple of times.

"Where in God's name have you been?" my mother exploded and you could tell by her voice that she was both mad but relieved too. "It's gone midnight and you've got school in the morning!"

I opened my mouth to answer but could find nothing to say. I certainly couldn't tell her the truth.

"He looks hurt," Nana Sara said and at that moment Mum made a sort of gagging sound as she breathed in and swallowed simultaneously. She stepped forward to look at me more closely.

"Mum..." I winced with the pain in my ankle as I instinctively leaned away but she was staring at my face.

"Have you been fighting?"

Again I felt my jaws open like I had something to say but there was nothing except the same sorry squeak I had made when Jay had his hand round my throat.

Mum took my head in her hands, angling my face to the light. I suddenly became aware of the throbbing in my temple, where I had cracked my head on the car window, much earlier in the evening. She led me through to the kitchen, my grandmother scurrying off to fetch disinfectant and fill a soup bowl with hot water.

"Adie, you tell me right this instant what kind of trouble you've got yourself into," demanded my mother. "You tell me right now."

My brain was so frazzled I couldn't even come up with a convincing lie. I just knew that she didn't really want to hear the truth, whatever she was saying. My eyelids were hot and heavy but the rest of me was cold and shivery. My limbs ached. The backs of my legs smarted. My ankle twinged.

"I got jumped by some guys," I said finally as Mum helped me into a kitchen chair. Both my mother and my grandmother inhaled sharply. "They had me up against a wall." My hand went automatically to my throat. It was only half a lie after all.

"But why didn't you come home? Where have you been until midnight?"

"I don't know." I shook my head, a signal for them to stop with the inquisition, too tired to open my mouth and make sounds like proper words.

Mum dabbed at my face with the hot water and disinfectant. She took a hold of my hands and examined my knuckles as if expecting to see them scuffed and bleeding from the brawl but of course there was nothing and she let them go again. Perhaps she knew I was lying. Nana Sara made me a hot cup of sweet ginger tea.

"Do you need to see a doctor?" Mum asked in a strange voice and I shook my head. "Well what's wrong with your leg? I saw you limping back there."

"I twisted my ankle running away from them." I reached for my tea, glad to have something to hold onto.

I sensed the two of them looking at each other.

"I think I really just need to go to bed," I told them, wincing as I put weight back onto my bad foot. "I'm sorry I made you both worry."

"Well shouldn't we tell the police?" my mum asked.

"Tell them what?" I looked at her.

"I don't know; something so that they can catch whoever it was that mugged you, Adie, that's their *job*."

"Mum, people get jumped all the time. Besides, I didn't see their faces. I just want to forget it, okay?" I tried to look her in the eye but couldn't and I knew she suspected I hadn't been entirely truthful with her.

"We'll talk in the morning," she called after me and her words hung in the hallway like a threat.

Upstairs I slipped on my uncool pyjamas noticing a bruise on the back of one leg. As I pressed on it I realised I must have caught myself as Curtis pushed me off the park bench. That seemed too long ago for it all to be part of the same evening. I climbed stiffly between the bedcovers drawing them up around my neck as if it were the middle of winter. My head swam with everything that had happened, a montage of disjointed images. At least I wasn't thinking about my dad anymore.

The warmth from my bed came over me like the hot air rushing out of that tube tunnel. I felt like I was floating. I remembered the way Curtis made the stolen car take off through the air. This time though I don't remember coming back down to earth because I was already asleep.

"What are you doing Adie? What on earth *do you think you are doing?"*

Some time had passed but I couldn't tell how long. It certainly wasn't long enough. I tried to unstick my eyes but they wouldn't open.

"Adie! Answer me."

I could feel sleep sliding away from me now and reluctantly forced open one eye.

Someone was standing in the middle of my tiny room but it was still dark and it took a moment or two for my vision to find its focus through the blackness.

"Babu?" My grandfather had come back! He stood there once more in his favourite dark funeral suit. I scrabbled to sit upright. "What are you doing here?"

"I'm here because I'm worried about you, Adie."

"But you're…I mean we…" I sat very still for a moment. "This isn't happening, is it? I mean, not really." I kept staring at him but he remained impassive, his shadowy face turned towards me. "You're just a dream, right?"

"You're acting more and more like those no-good boys you hang out with," Babu scolded.

"I don't hang out with them," I corrected him. "Just once in a while."

"You think I don't see the way things are?"

"How can you? You're…" but again something stopped me from saying the word.

"Adie, you are a good boy, a smart boy. You can do so much more with your life, why are you so set on doing nothing?"

I shuffled back in my bed, catching the wall with my shoulder. I would have liked to put a bit more distance between us but, like I said before, mine is the box room, the smallest room in the house. There was a spiciness in the air again, a smell of something exotic, patchouli and sandalwood perhaps.

"Life is so precious," continued Babu. *"You'd do well to remember that. Take it from someone who has seen the last grain of sand fall through the hour-glass. The most wonderful possibilities are still out there for you."*

"Sure, I'm going to be a brain surgeon some day," I mumbled into my pyjamas.

"And why not be a brain surgeon if that's what you truly want?" asked Babu.

"Right now all I want is some sleep." I flexed my shoulder and a pain shot down my side.

"You never used to be so disrespectful," my grandfather noted coldly.

"And you never used to be so dead," I mumbled back. Finally.

He paused, but didn't move, just kept staring at me. *"When you die you close the last door, Adie. Don't be so quick to close doors in life. Listen to me. Listen to me!"*

"I am, all right? Jeez!" I peeked over at him, drawing my knees up under the bedclothes for protection. I didn't feel as brave as I sounded.

"We all have choices. But they run out the more doors you close."

Behind him there was a knocking sound and Mum peeped her head in.

"You okay? I thought I heard you talking to someone."

"Yeah, no, I'm okay." I shuffled gingerly back down.

"You sure? It's too late for phone calls."

"It wasn't that." I moved my head on the pillow. "It was just a bad dream."

"You want me to sit with you?" she asked and as much as I did just then I had to tell her no.

"Hey Mum, can you just leave the door open a bit?"

"Sure." She pushed it a little wider, letting in a triangle of yellow light from the landing. "Get some sleep and we'll talk in the morning."

It still sounded like a threat. But not as empty as my room. Babu was gone.

CHAPTER EIGHT

"You weren't in school yesterday," Cara noted.

"What are you, the truancy officer?"

"I'm just saying, how come you weren't in school?"

I shook my head. "If I tell you, I'll have to kill you."

"Curtis Laycock wasn't in registration yesterday either. I guess you were with him again, huh?"

I grimaced, not ready to discuss this with her. Mum had grilled me enough as it was. She had taken the morning off work to do it properly.

I was glad Curtis still wasn't in school today so at least I didn't have to think any more about Sunday night. Then I started to worry that the reason no one had seen him since the weekend was that the cops had got him. And if they had got *him,* then it was only a matter of time before they got me too. By first break I had worked myself into a real state over it.

There was still no sign of him by chucking-out time and I was starting to panic. I caught sight of PeeWee over by the front gates and called to him but as soon as he saw me he took off in the opposite direction and I didn't dare run after him in case it really was as bad as I was imagining. Instead I walked home with Cara and Paul, turning down Paul's offer of mucking about on his keyboard for an hour or two because Mum had expressly forbidden any 'dawdling' as she called it. She wanted me straight home from now on, she had told me yesterday. And that wasn't all.

"You need to get yourself a job," she announced over dinner that night.

"What d'you mean? What about school?"

"After school. For the summer," she said. "It'll give you a sense of purpose, keep you out of trouble."

"Mum, I keep telling you, I'm not in any trouble."

"Hanging round the streets for six weeks, nothing to do." She wasn't exactly talking to me, more to herself or Nana Sara who just nodded, thinking of elephants and a man who once sold bolts of brightly coloured cloth. "Maybe one of your uncles can find you a job."

"I'm not spending the summer in some boring old shop!"

"Well you're not spending the summer hanging round the streets like a hoodlum either." She sounded quite adamant about that and I knew better than to argue the point.

All of a sudden, I could see six glorious weeks of summer holidays vaporising before my eyes: I would spend it stuck behind the desk at my uncle Tyrone's photo framing business or running errands for Tito who spends his life unlocking mobile phones and wiring money to far flung corners of the globe. Or maybe I was destined to help out in the textiles shop with Mum's oldest brother, Harry, and his wife Didi.

"I'm not going to let you throw your life away like all the other boys round here," said Mum with a determined look in her eyes. "That's not how you were raised, Adie."

I opened my mouth to give her one of my whip-sharp comebacks but she silenced me with that death-stare of hers. I swear down, she must have been bitten by a radioactive spider once, and that is her super-power: the ability to suck the words right out of you.

And there was so much I *could* have said: yes mum, remind me again how I was I raised: in the back of tour buses?; with dad partying his face off all night long in the next room?; on planes and in the backseats of limos, always going to somewhere or from somewhere, meeting him between gigs, between deals, between contracts, between parties and fancy hotel rooms? The way I was raised wasn't so different to anyone else round here when you scratched below the surface. Curtis Laycock had said it fine: I was just another kid with a deadbeat dad.

    For the next couple of days if I wasn't going to or from school, I wasn't going anywhere. Mum was not budging on this. She was keeping a very close eye on me from now on, she reckoned.

    "You can come to the supermarket with me," she announced brightly on Saturday, as if she was doing me a favour.

    "What do I want to do that for?"

    Nana Sara scowled at my bad manners but didn't say anything.

    "You can help me with the shopping," said Mum like that was an acceptable answer. "I thought you would be going stir-crazy by now."

    I wasn't, but I also knew better than to turn down her demand-disguised-as-an-offer.

    Outside the sun was hot, baking the grey pavements of east London and filling the normally dull streets with light and colour and laughter. Everyone always seems happier when the sun is shining. I walked alongside my mother, hoping no one would see me from school, being dragged round the shops like a little kid.

"So, what are you reading these days, Adie?" asked Mum in an attempt to make conversation.

I shrugged. "This and that, you know."

She laughed to herself. "You always did that as a child too, always read two or three books at a time. Always had your nose in at least two books."

"Maybe I'll be a librarian when I leave school then," I muttered sourly. "Would that make you happy?"

"When was the last time you went into a library?" she asked me. "Libraries are dying out. Your internet generation has killed them all off."

We walked into Pearson Street. It is lined with small shops: a pawnbroker's and a Poundland, a cash-converters and a Café Nero with tables arranged out on the pavement, a Greggs bakery and a key-cutters and shoe-repair place that always smells of glue. Sitting on the pavement by the shoe-place was a thin looking man with long wavy brown hair held in position by a headband, like the hippies used to wear back in the olden days. He was wearing a shaggy sheepskin coat despite the heat and in his hand was one massive great cone. I did a double-take at that because even round here you can't be quite that open about your drug-taking. His glazed eyes instantly locked onto mine.

"Dude, put that away!" I muttered as Mum and I walked passed him.

"Man, I'm so cold I can't move," he groaned.

"It's summer, you stoner. Get a life!" I muttered back over my shoulder.

"Sorry?" Mum turned to look at me.

I shook my head. "That guy there..." And I knew from the suspicious look on her face that there was no guy, or if there was, *she* couldn't see him. I flicked my eyes back to the pavement where he had been sitting not five seconds ago and a familiar sick feeling settled deep inside my gut like an acid-flavoured milkshake.

"Look Adie, I know you're mad at me right now," Mum sighed, "But until you can prove to me that I don't have to worry about you anymore, you are going to be on a very short leash!" I opened my mouth to try and explain but she held a bony finger in front of my face. "No more back-chat. This is not open to discussion, young man."

We walked on in silence. My head pounded with a sudden headache. What did it mean to be seeing things that no one else could? Maybe I had a brain tumour. I decided to Google it as soon as we got back.

My nerves were already shredded with my impending brain tumour so when the doorbell rang at lunchtime that same day and I found two people that looked like coppers standing there I very nearly had a heart-attack as well. I took a couple of steps back from the door. Mum and Nana Sara were already coming out of the kitchen, dabbing at the remains of lunch from their mouths.

"Mum, I…" I had no idea how I was going to continue that sentence apart from 'it wasn't my fault' but even inside my head that sounded lame.

Mum was looking at one of the officers now and I turned back to see he was holding out a small colour photograph of a boy aged three or four years old. My mind and heart raced but I stood there without moving until Mum nudged me out of the way, a funny look on her face.

"Sorry to bother you," started the community support officer as I imagined myself holding out my wrists for them to slap the cuffs onto, "we're just going door to door asking people if they have seen this little boy." I forced my eyes to look again at the picture he held out for the three of us. It wasn't me. Or Curtis. It was some little kid I had never seen before. "His name is Milo Petranovic," said the officer. "He lives in Enderby Street but hasn't been seen now for the last twenty-four hours."

Mum took the picture and studied it hard before passing it over to my grandmother who did the same. They were both making sympathetic noises, I just heard odd words – 'oh…terrible…poor baby…his parents …frantic…' – as my mind tried to process the fact that I wasn't actually being arrested.

"We're asking people to look in any sheds or outhouses, you know, and just keep an eye out for him," said the PCSO. "He's wearing a red Paw Patrol sweatshirt and blue jeans."

"Yes, yes of course," my mother nodded as Nana Sara handed back the photograph, frowning hard at me as she did so. "We'll certainly keep our eyes open."

We closed the door as they moved to the next house and through the wood I could hear them rattling our neighbour's letterbox.

"Poor little boy." Mum walked back to the kitchen. "Let's hope they find him before any harm comes his way."

Nana Sara narrowed her eyes at me as I sloped past her. "You look sick there, Adie. Ah, if I didn't know you better, I'd think you believed they came looking for you."

"You're chatting nonsense, Nana. They weren't even real police." I fell back into my seat at the kitchen table. "I got a headache is all. I think it's a brain tumour."

"Brain tumour indeed!" Mum picked up her fork. "Don't be using that as an excuse to get out of cooking dinner tonight."

CHAPTER NINE

The last Friday of every month my father picks me up and I spend the weekend with him at his house in north London. Usually we just play computer games or watch box sets on Netflix. Sometimes he brings out the guitars and tries to get me to jam with him but that's not as much fun as it sounds. This Friday, though, he was going to be in court.

"I don't want to go over there," I told my mum a couple of nights before. "I don't want to see him."

She looked concerned. "You love going over there. I thought you'd jump at the chance after being cooped up in the house with me and Nana for so long."

I shrugged. "I *don't* love going over there and anyway, what's the point? He's probably just going to be in jail."

"Adie!" She made a sucking noise. "Don't talk like that. Your dad will be so disappointed if you don't go."

"No he won't. Besides, I don't care how he feels."

Mum followed me into the kitchen and stood there as I banged a few cupboard doors in an attempt to feel better, looking for something to eat. "What is it? Talk to me."

"What's to say? I don't want to spend the weekend with him. Big deal."

"He's your father."

"Yeah, well he should have thought about that when he was on his last bender, shouldn't he?" And I stomped up to my room to listen to Eminem loud enough to make my point.

As it turned out, he didn't get put in jail. Mum said that this good fortune was largely thanks to John Parker, who we already knew was an ace legal-eagle, and also thanks to Dad's long-suffering PA: a red-headed lady called Becky Frazer. They both vouched for his otherwise good character and the fact that he hadn't had an "episode" like the one which saw him tearing drunkenly through the streets in a stolen limo for several years now. Apparently, John was personally seeing to it that dad went back into rehab but I told Mum I still didn't care. My father could do what the hell he liked, just as he always had.

And true to form, with a total disregard for my wishes, he turned up on our doorstep Saturday morning despite a long tense phone call with my mother the night before when she had broken the news to him that I hadn't wanted to visit this month. When I heard the hammering on the door my first thought was that he was drunk again and all manner of emotions churned dangerously inside me. Mostly I was angry. He didn't even have the sense to stay away. It had never mattered to him what *I* wanted and here was the proof. Again.

"Adie, mate!" he cried spotting me at the top of the stairs as Mum ushered him quickly inside.

He's a big man, six foot and then some, broad too, though he's a bit more stooped now, older than his years from all the partying he did in his youth. His hair is blond and shaggy, down past his shoulders. Today he had it tied back in a neat pony tail. He took off his sunglasses and hung them round the neck of his t-shirt, which was old and black and had 'Guns 'n'

Roses' written on the front and a load of tour dates on the back. The only time I ever see him in a proper shirt is when he has a court appearance, or that time in LA when they collected an award for best rock band, all dressed up in glittery suits. Dad always wears jewellery too. One of his ears is pierced and today a small silver skull was swinging from it, matching the skull rings on his fingers. Two sleeves of tattoos cover the whites of his arms. He doesn't exactly look like a regular dad, but then again he's not a regular dad; never has been.

"I missed you last night," he told me.

I stood there, rooted by my anger, three steps from the top. Eventually the smile faded from his face as he realised I wasn't coming down and he allowed himself to be steered into the kitchen by my mother.

"How have you been anyway?" he asked her and I sank down onto the stairs to listen, just as I had when I was seven years old and the rows were starting.

I could hear Mum bustling round the kitchen fixing him some tea telling him he shouldn't have come but keeping her voice low so that I couldn't always make out what she was saying.

"I'm worried about him…" she whispered and I leaned my head to the bannisters. "…so secretive…"

"Of course boys that age are gonna have secrets from their mums," Dad replied easily. "Trust me, you don't want to know what he's doing half the time!"

"…more than that," she said. "I'm worried what he gets up to when he's out of the house."

"You want me to have a word with him?" Dad asked and I heard my mother sigh long and hard.

"You saw him, Craig. Right now you're the last person he wants to talk to. He's angry with you most of all."

"Me? What have I done?" wailed Dad.

I could imagine my mother giving him that exasperated look of hers. "When you go out and get drunk and start fights it affects all of us," she said, louder now.

"When you have a child it's not just about *you* anymore. I'd hope after fifteen years you might have realised that. What do you think it does to him to read about his drunken father in the newspapers the next day?"

"It was one relapse," my father mumbled. "Besides, what they said in the papers, half that stuff was made up!"

"I don't care. One relapse is still one too many. I'm just saying, try to see it from his point of view for once."

I held my breath waiting for his reply.

"Yeah, you're probably right," he sighed eventually. "You always were smarter than me. God knows how we ever got together, eh?"

If Mum had said something to that, I couldn't hear it. There was a long silence, presumably as they both drank their tea. Then the voices started again, low and conspiratorial. I wanted to hear what they were saying but I was damned if I was going to show the slightest bit of interest for him. Finally, I heard the scraping back of chairs so I sprang to my feet and hopped back to my bedroom, pressing the door quietly shut behind me. Part of me wanted him to come up here and beg me to spend the weekend with him but another part of me just wanted him out of the house and when he didn't come up the stairs I was disappointed, as I knew I would be, as much with myself as with him.

CHAPTER TEN

I couldn't be sure whose idea it was, but I can tell you one thing: it wasn't mine. Mum sat me down the following weekend – just two weeks before we were due to break up from school – and asked what I had done about getting a job. She knew damn well I had done nothing.

"Well, Adie, your father and I may have come up with an alternative," she smiled and I got the feeling I had been led into a deliberate trap. "How would you like to spend the summer with him in Norfolk?"

"Norfolk? What the hell's in Norfolk?"

Mum kept her face expressionless, though I got the feeling it wasn't easy. "It turns out that John Parker's family have a house there and he thought it would do your father good to get away from everything for a while, you know, away from all the usual..." and she paused, choosing her last word carefully, "...distractions."

"And what's that got to do with me?" I shrugged.

"Well, we all thought it would be nice for you and him to spend some quality time together, one on one." She looked at me, a smile frozen onto her lips. "What do you think?"

I scratched at my arms, shrugged. "Sounds like a stupid idea to me."

"Well if you still think you are going to spend six weeks just hanging round the streets with your mates, you are very much mistaken mister," she reminded me.

I shrugged again. "Fine. Pack me off to Norfolk. See if I care." And I stomped out of the room.

"Fine. Norfolk it is," she called after me.

"Fine!"

"Fine!" she yelled back, this time determined to have the last word.

I Googled Norfolk only to discover it was very flat and very empty looking, with lots of marsh lands and fens and quaint, tiny villages. It might be a good place to spend your holiday if you were, like, seventy and close to death but otherwise I couldn't see there was a whole lot going for it. And now I was spending the summer there with my deadbeat dad, watching him dry out and make more promises that I knew he would never keep. Working in Tyrone's picture-framing shop seemed almost tempting.

Cara's solution was simple: just refuse to go.

"Are you serious?" I gagged. "You know what my mum is like when she gets an idea in her head."

"Maybe it won't be so bad," she shrugged.

"And maybe it will be horrible."

"We'll all come and visit. For a wild party," Paul promised.

I looked at him. He had never been to a wild party in his life. His idea of a party still included jelly, ice-cream and paper hats.

"It's in the middle of nowhere," I told them. "And I mean *literally* in the middle of nowhere. It's like a six-mile hike to the nearest village."

"Why are they sending you off to the middle of nowhere?" asked Paul.

"So that I can *bond* with my dad," I groaned. "God! It's going to be the worst summer ever!"

And so it was that on July 27th a giant black Hummer pulled up outside our house and my father bounded out of it like a puppy escaping its leash. I watched him from my window as he hammered enthusiastically on our front door making a few net curtains twitch along the street. Mum pulled him inside.

"He'll be down in a minute," I heard her say. "What's with the car? You couldn't get something more, I don't know, more *ordinary*?"

"It's John's, he's driving us. Hey! There he is!" He leapt up the stairs to help with the large suitcase which I was now lugging down one step at a time.

I shoved it towards him and he stumbled backwards with a grunt, only just managing to catch himself against the wall and stop from falling the rest of the way down. "What have you got in here, kid, the kitchen sink?"

Hearing the commotion, Nana Sara came through and stood in the hallway, her eyes narrowing as she scanned him for illicit substances, stumbling around like that, just like the old days. He righted himself and half threw the giant suitcase down to the bottom.

"My iPad's in there. Be careful will you?" I complained.

"IPad? You think there'll be internet where we're going?" he laughed.

"You better be joking me, man," I growled coming down the stairs into Mum's embarrassingly suffocating hug.

"I'm sure it'll be fine, Adie." She kissed me over and over, making me squirm to get away. "I will miss you *so* much!"

"Can I come home if it's crap then?" I asked her and thought I saw a look shoot between her and my father.

"Of course," she whispered.

Then it was Nana Sara's turn and I was once more smothered in kisses, choking on her old-fashioned perfume. "You be a good boy," she warned.

"*Both* of you be good boys," my mother threatened looking between me and my father.

"I'll look after him, don't you worry," smiled Dad but my mum's face told me exactly what she thought of his promises.

Out at the car John Parker was standing by the open back door. He helped Dad haul my case along the wide seat.

"The boot's already full," he explained. "Your dad still thinks he's on tour with a road crew to lug his kit around for him."

"What d'you want me to do for the next month?" asked Dad. "Play Dominoes?"

John Parker stood back and looked at me. "You've grown tall, Adie. Last time I saw you, you were this high." And he held his hand out level with his stomach.

I shrugged, not sure what I was supposed to say. Thanks? I didn't really get much say in the whole getting taller thing, like so many other parts of my life. I hopped up into the back of the car alongside my case as Mum and Nana Sara came out to wave us off. My mum shook her head again at the obscene size of the vehicle. My father doesn't do incognito.

I settled back and stuffed the earbuds into my ears just so I wouldn't be expected to make conversation but as soon as John started the engine the vehicle was filled with music anyway. It was a Voodoo Mary track. I didn't bother switching on my tunes, but I didn't remove the earbuds either.

"I always liked this track," John was saying. "Has an African beat to it in there somewhere."

"Yeah, that's where my head was at, back then," Dad shouted over his former self belting out the lyrics to 'Desert Princess'. "That was the beginning of the end if you ask me. I wanted to go in a more ethnic direction and Stu was rocking that whole death metal vibe. Hard to fuse the two. Artistic differences."

I snorted to myself. Artistic differences my arse. Dad and all the others were permanently baked out of their brains by this time. Something had to give sooner or later, but I figured if Dad wanted to call it artistic differences, then let him.

The Sat-Nav on the dashboard directed John to the motorway and soon we had left the Capital far behind. I watched the scenery whizzing by and felt like a little kid all over again, something about backseats and being taken places that you're not exactly sure you want to go to.

Once we were off the motorway, we stopped for lunch at a roadside café where John's car drew admiring glances from our fellow diners. One of them even recognised my father and got him to autograph a ketchup-smeared napkin. Dad was loving it as usual. Eventually they stopped looking at us and we were able to order our food.

"I've taken the liberty of doing an online shop for you. Should be enough to last you through the first week at least." John looked up from his phone, texting and talking and ordering off the big plastic menu, all at the same time. "You owe me one-hundred-and-twenty-seven pounds by the way. The omelette, are the eggs free-range?" He looked up at the server who said she would find out and disappeared back to the kitchen. John glanced over at my father. "Mrs Dodds, the cleaner, comes once a week, you know, to keep the place aired. She'll have sorted out the delivery but we'll stop in the local village for anything else. Just don't, well, you know. Just try and keep the place as if only the *one* bomb's gone off, okay?"

"Scouts honour," smiled Dad.

The server came back and said yes, they were free-range eggs so John ordered a cheese omelette and chips. "Becky will stop by in a couple of days, just to check on you both." John glanced across at me, then to my dad, then to me again. "You'll have a great time."

My face made it pretty obvious that I didn't share his enthusiasm. I grimaced at the girl with her pad and pencil and ordered a double cheeseburger and fries. I figured what Mum didn't know wouldn't hurt her. Or me. The server was now looking at my father, who is a bit indecisive ever since the drugs burned a hole in his brain. The menu quivered in his hands.

"It'll be good to get back to basics," John was saying. "Fresh air, clean living. You could do a bit of fishing, walking, cycling, whatever you fancy."

"Great," I muttered. "How about none of the above?"

"Back to basics," he nodded at my father.

"No sex, no drugs, just the rock 'n' roll. I get it," said Dad.

At this point the girl twigged who he was. "OMG!" she exclaimed. "You're that guy from Voodoo

Mary." Dad beamed up at her. "My boyfriend's father is like totally into your music."

Dad ordered fish and chips and watched as she sashayed back across the floor to the kitchens, presumably to text her boyfriend about the VIP she had just served. Then Dad slumped forward and put his head in both hands.

"God, I feel old!"

With our bellies full and the car gassed up, we were on the move again, heading further and further away from civilisation. We left the last big town behind and ventured out into a flat, grassy landscape that stretched on forever, flattened under the weight of an immense and unending sky.

"If I've overlooked anything, I'm sure Becky can sort it out when she comes down," John said. "You know we're both here for you. From now on, she's reporting directly back to me!"

"Is there internet there?" I leaned forward in my seat, almost not daring to ask.

"It's not the best connection in the world, but yeah," he answered. "I updated everything a year or two ago, put in a new modem so I could work from home if I chose. I'll write down the code for you."

"And mobiles?"

"Not so great," he said and I slumped miserably back in my seat.

"The whole idea is *not* to be disturbed by the outside world," Dad pointed out.

"But what if we have an emergency?" I demanded. "What if I get a brain tumour or something?"

Dad guffawed with laughter. "Brain tumour! We'll send up a smoke signal, Adie. Someone will see it eventually."

"I'm serious!" The idea of being trapped in a house in the middle of nowhere for any length of time with my lunatic father and no way of summoning help did not sit well with me.

"There's a landline," John Parker assured me. "It's not exactly the dark ages out there."

"Are you sure about that?"

After another forty minutes of twisting and turning along narrow country lanes John stopped the car. We were in what I suppose passed for a village: there was a single post office-cum-shop and a small thatched pub called The Green Man along with a scatter of houses. The sign on the grass verge said Lower Huffingham. I loitered outside the shop checking for a mobile signal and wondered if Upper Huffingham would be any better while John and my father bought extra milk and a few other provisions. Then we were back in the car again and even the houses disappeared from sight. Field after empty field stretched before us. At one point I saw a windmill, then nothing else for absolutely ages.

Eventually John slowed the car and we turned (somewhat awkwardly given its immense size) through a set of rusty iron gates.

"This is it," he announced and I craned my neck to see what 'it' might be – but there was still nothing except a long winding lane with trees on either side.

We passed the crumbling remains of what at one time might have been a coach house and then the lane opened out to reveal an enormous L-shaped building, ivy climbing up its stone walls and ugly gargoyles leering down on us from below a steep slate roof. Dad let out a string of expletives as he saw them, clearly impressed.

"How is it I never came here before?" He stepped out of the car into the shadows of the imposing house. "It woulda made a great location for one of our videos!"

We all gazed up at the grand stone building with its grotesque demonic creatures eyeing our every move. I must have shuddered because John clapped a hand warmly on my shoulder.

"Don't worry. They were originally built to deflect the rain water off the masonry, nothing more sinister than that." He leaned into my ear. "And they also ward off evil spirits so, present company notwithstanding, you should be fine!"

I looked at their fat faces and heavy brows, leering toothy mouths, sharp ears and horns, creatures that were half-man half-beast and I wasn't entirely convinced.

"You actually own this?" I couldn't believe that one person, a non-musician regular-type person, could own a house that was clearly the size of a hotel.

"Yup." John shielded his eyes from the late afternoon sunlight. "Picked it up for a song in the last property crash."

"How come you don't live here then?"

"Oh, I don't know." He turned back to the car and opened the boot. "Never seemed the right time somehow. The likes of your old man kept me too busy in London, I guess, so I just never got round to it."

"It's not haunted, is it?" I asked him.

He pulled one of my father's bags from the boot. "Course it is. Built way back in the sixteen-hundreds, it's got to have picked up a ghost or two along the way, isn't that right Craig?"

My dad made a low, moaning noise and raised his tattooed arms, zombie-style. Yeah, this was going to be a barrel of laughs.

I looked into the boot noticing how much stuff he had brought with him. There was a laptop, a guitar, keyboards and two amps, a couple of games consoles, a box of games, another of DVDs and magazines, an old-style ghetto blaster, a plastic carrier of shoes, a bag of vitamins and supplements, some other random bags and a big open rucksack of clothes even though he always looks the same, day in day out. And he had the nerve to accuse me of bringing the kitchen sink? He'd brought the fridge and the oven too.

"You could help your old man, you know," he muttered taking hold of the rucksack and throwing it in the general direction of the main entrance.

He handed me his keyboard and we followed John up to the doorway, waiting as he unlocked the heavy wooden door. Dad and I followed him inside to a wide entrance hall that smelled faintly of damp.

"This place needs someone to live in it for a while. You can tell no one's been here for years apart from Mrs Dodds and she's so old I'm not entirely sure she's not dead herself."

Directly in front of the main door, across the brown and yellow tiled hallway, was a wide wood-panelled staircase. The paint on the walls above the panelling was patchy where once upon a time pictures must have hung. To either side of us, left and right, were two great doors leading on to the various downstairs rooms.

"Me and Adie will breathe some fresh life into this old house, won't we, son?" Dad grinned, clearly imagining the wild parties he could have in a place like this. (Unlike my friend Paul, my father *does* know how to have a wild party.) "Open a few windows, get that stuffy old-people's home stink out of it." He dropped his bags down on the floor and looked around.

I placed the keyboard gently on top of an ornate, wooden chair.

"Don't sit on that," warned John, "it's two-hundred years old – more for show than sitting on."

He was standing in front of a grandfather clock. He glanced at me, then down at his watch, repositioning the hands on the old clock face accordingly.

"You'll need to do this every two or three days," he instructed as he began to laboriously wind it over and over. "The key is kept inside here."

He paused to listen for a moment as it started to steadily thunk out the time. It seemed like a lot of bother when you could just peek at your phone. Satisfied, he moved into the first reception room to our left, with my father and I trotting obediently behind. Dad swore his appreciation. The ceilings were crazy high with all this decorative coving around the edges and you know the first thing that came to my mind? How would you ever reach up there to get a cobweb down? Clearly living most of my life with Mum and Nana Sara had rubbed off on me. Badly. Maybe a bit of time with my father was not such a mistake after all.

John pulled off the sheets from the furniture to reveal a large sofa and a couple of armchairs all in some kind of flowery material that was probably really expensive but which I wouldn't have given house-room to if this had been *my* crib. At least there was a huge flat-screen TV in here, but other than that the room seemed to be trapped in a time warp. Then John lead us through the eight-foot door at the far end and we found ourselves in what was intended to be the dining room. John whisked away more white sheeting to uncover a highly polished dining table and chairs, all very formal looking.

"Jeeves, pass the salt would you? Chop chop!" said Dad in a mock-snooty voice.

John Parker moved to the windows and threw back the curtains some more. A shaft of sunlight caught the millions of dust motes floating in the musty air and Dad coughed.

"Like I said, it'll do this house good to have someone living in it for more than a weekend at a time," said John. "We had the best of intentions when we bought it but…" and his voice trailed off.

"I'm definitely paying you too much," muttered Dad as John took us through another door which in turn led to a corridor and a kitchen as big as some people's whole flats.

I was pleased to see that as well as the old oak table in the middle and the copper pans hanging from rails suspended from the ceiling and the old range (which may or may not have also been just for show) there was a modern fridge the size of a spaceship, a microwave, a cooker and a load of Tesco carrier bags crammed behind the kitchen bin, which I took to mean there was proper, edible, modern food somewhere in this house.

The kitchen opened onto a conservatory and beyond that there were lawns and trees and more trees and more lawns.

"Oh, and Phil the gardener also comes in once or twice a week," John said to no one in particular. We followed him back round to the other wing as he pointed out things of interest. "Downstairs cloakroom." He opened a door and we were hit by the smell of bleach and air freshener. He closed it again. "Phone. Numbers are in that book there. Fuse box." He stopped and looked up at it. "It trips sometimes so you may need to reset it every once in a while. No major shakes. There are always candles and matches in the kitchen for when the power is down."

Dad waved his silver skull rings dismissively at John Parker's concerns. "Remember I was an electrician in my former life. I think I can manage a few dodgy electrics, thank you very much."

"Nothing dodgy here," John corrected him. "Had the whole place rewired about two years ago."

"We'll be fine, won't we Adie?" Dad winked at me.

"Well, you can certainly play your music as loud as you like," smiled John, "no neighbours are going to complain, that's for sure."

There were three more rooms in the other wing, equally spacious as the ones we had just seen, with the same high ceilings and draughty windows with heavy floor length curtains, which John now threw open as we passed.

"I asked Mrs Dodds to air the place," he mumbled. "She must have forgotten."

At the end of the wing was another wood-panelled staircase, this one slightly narrower than the one in the hall. We followed John up the creaking wooden steps and found ourselves in a long, dark, carpeted hallway.

"There are ten bedrooms in all," he announced opening a couple of doors to show us, letting in shafts of much-needed light, "so you can pretty much sleep wherever. Hell, you could sleep in a different room every night of the week if you wanted. There are beds and furniture in most of them. We inherited most of the stuff from the previous owners. Sheets and blankets are in this cupboard here." He pulled open another door to reveal a walk-in cupboard stacked to the ceiling with blankets and sheets and pillows and duvets. "I got Mrs Dodds to make up a couple of beds in the biggest rooms for you, but if you don't like them, well..." he looked back down the corridor, "simply choose somewhere else."

"I have to sleep with my feet facing Mecca," said Dad. "It's my new thaang."

John Parker cocked an eyebrow. "It's that way." And he pointed randomly.

My father is not as funny as he thinks he is; spend too much time with him and you grow pretty tired of his so-called sense of humour.

It took ages to unload the car and bring all of Dad's stuff in. Eventually though we were done and John dragged my father outside saying he needed a 'quick word' in private so I left them out the front of the house and went and sat on a chair in the hall that was hopefully not two-hundred years old and not just for show.

My being here still didn't feel real. It was so far away from my old life in east London, Mum and Nana Sara, Paul, Cara, Curtis... Curtis would do his nut if he could see this place but it was hard to picture him here, as if they had all become characters from a TV show I had seen once, many moons ago. Maybe that was what Mum was counting on. I had a sudden over-riding urge to talk to her, to assure myself that my old life was still there, and I looked at the antiquated phone on the little round table to my side. Maybe it would be better to use the more modern cordless one in John's office, I thought, but I felt like I should ask permission first, whichever phone I used, so I pulled out my mobile instead – but of course there was no signal.

I hovered in the doorway as John Parker gave my dad what sounded like an extensive list of do's and don'ts. Dad was doing a lot of nodding and looking around him like he was being told off. It was odd to watch, odd to remember that my father has this whole entourage of people looking out for him, doing things for him, pulling empty stately homes out of their hats for him just to keep him out of trouble. Being as angry with him as I often was, I sometimes forgot just how famous he still is.

Finally, he came back into the hallway and shut the door behind him. It seemed to suck itself closed as if sealing in a vacuum. The grandfather clock ticked slowly, annoyingly, but other than that it was absolutely silent. I wasn't used to this level of quiet.

"Well, that's that then," said my father and I guess we both felt the awkwardness between us, with no one else around to act as a buffer.

Dad looked up and down the hallway, at the spread of bags and boxes and electronic equipment sprawling over the tiled floor. I suddenly realised how long the summer holiday really was and felt a wave of homesickness rise up from my gut.

"Best get these upstairs, eh?" Dad grabbed a bag and smiled uneasily at me.

Once he had gone I put my head in my hands and wondered how the hell either of us was going to survive.

CHAPTER ELEVEN

As if to emphasize the massive proportions of this house, Mrs Dodds had allocated us rooms at opposite ends of the two corridors. My room looked out over the back lawn with its wall of trees in the far distance. Dad's bedroom overlooked the forecourt and the long winding lane that led down to the road. There were also two bathrooms up here, one for each wing, so in effect we both had our own self-contained suites. Dad was probably used to living like this but for me, well, it all felt pretty weird.

I had a four-poster double bed to myself which I launched myself onto as soon as I was alone, pleasantly surprised with the springiness of the thick mattress. There was also a dark wooden wardrobe with a long oval mirror on one door – which threw back embarrassing reflections of myself bouncing on the bed like a little kid – as well as a tall chest of drawers and two bedside tables. I soon realised I hadn't brought enough stuff as, even after I'd emptied out the entire contents of my huge suitcase, there were still drawers and shelves left empty. Even the furniture was bigger than I was used to. I rearranged things, trying to take up as much space as I could.

Much later I found Dad in the kitchen as the dregs of the afternoon paled into evening and hunger drew us together again. He was standing looking blankly into the spaceship-sized fridge.

"Suppose we should start thinking about dinner," he said and you could tell from the worried tone of his voice that he had absolutely no idea how to go about doing that.

I opened a few cupboards. They were stuffed full of tins and packets and the walk-in pantry revealed boxes and bags of fresh fruit and vegetables. At least, in theory, we weren't going to starve.

"Should have brought a cook-book with us," Dad mumbled forlornly.

"There's recipes on the internet," I shrugged, watching him mooch aimlessly round the vast kitchen. He finally found something to do, reaching for the kettle and filling it with water. The tap gurgled and spluttered the way old plumbing sometimes does. "We'll make a cup of tea, eh? You want tea? I'll find some matches." His eyes cast about wildly in their search. I watched him for a moment, then went up to the stove and flicked it on.

"It's not gas. How would they get gas all the way out here?"

Dad looked at me as if I had just performed a magic trick. "Oh yeah, that's how that works. Nice one, Adie. Tea coming up." And I got that sinking feeling the way I always do when I spend too much time with my father.

Maybe once upon a time, before I was born, he lived like normal people did, but ever since Voodoo Mary topped the charts across the globe he's had people to call on to do absolutely everything for him. There was nothing he couldn't get just from picking up the phone. He hadn't had to look after himself in years; and he'd certainly never had to look after me.

"We could just open a tin," I suggested as he completed a second aimless lap of the kitchen.

He nodded but then shook his head. "No, I promised your mother. Fresh air, fresh food, the whole kit and caboodle." He found some mugs, then went back to the fridge for milk. "We're gonna cook proper food, mate, like I know you do at home. Hey, we could even catch it first, you know, out there…" And he nodded his head towards the window and the wilds of Norfolk beyond.

My father has never had too keen a grip on reality. In his drug-addled brain he had jumped from tinned soup to successfully bringing down a live deer, skinning it and then cooking it on a fire that he would no doubt have made himself by rubbing two sticks together. I just stared at him.

"Catch it with what? Your bare hands?" He pulled a milk carton from the spaceship. "Or did you bring a gun with you as well as everything else?"

Dad frowned. "Hey, I'm a lover not a fighter!"

I turned away. "You're an idiot is what you are." I said it quietly, safe in the knowledge that years of rock and roll had eroded his hearing. "Don't think I'm cooking dinner for you every night for five weeks." I added, a bit louder, turning back to him as he popped tea-bags into the mugs with a look of self-satisfaction on his face: he could at least make us a hot drink. Yippee. I wondered how soon I could call my mother and tell her I wanted to come home.

In the end it was me who made us both dinner that evening with Dad hovering, trying to help in his own bumbling, clueless way, learning what normal folk had to do to make food magically appear on the table. I cooked us spaghetti bolognaise opting for something that was safe and easy (though I was sorely tempted to make him the hottest curry I could manage with the ingredients to hand and blow his intestines out on our first night together). We ate in the dining room, symbolically sitting at opposite ends of the long dining table, sending the salt and pepper shakers skating down the polished wood to one another like air hockey pucks. We had to stop, though, when Dad let the salt slip off his end and as it hit the carpet, the silver top came off, spilling white stuff everywhere.

"I'll snort that up, don't worry," he grinned and I scowled and shook my head. "No, Jeeves will clean it up, won't you Jeeves?" Dad looked around for his imaginary butler then sucked up more spaghetti, grinning at me. "Man, I feel like I'm on the set of some crazy old movie."

The salt would probably stay on the carpet until I got a dustpan and brush.

We finished our meal and then discovered that in a house this size, one thing they didn't have was a dishwasher. Dad was incensed and ranted for five minutes while I filled the sink with suds and waited for him to get over the terrible injustice he'd just been dealt.

"And don't say Jeeves is gonna do it," I warned him as he stopped to draw breath. "You and I both know there ain't no Jeeves. And *I* cooked so that makes this *your* job. That's how it works."

"What about John's doddery old cleaner?"

"He said she only comes once a week."

Dad reluctantly slipped the chunky silver rings off his fingers, slowly, one at a time, delaying the inevitable, and no doubt hoping I would offer to do it for him in the meantime. I stood there as he lined his jewellery carefully to one side of the sink and I stayed there till he had dunked both his hands sullenly into the hot water.

I left him grumbling and mumbling to himself and went and sat in the conservatory, watching the sun turning the evening sky pink, then mauve. You could hear the crows cackling and cawing to each other as they started to settle down for the night. I'd never heard or seen so many birds before. Nana Sara would have loved it. They kept flying from one tree top to another, as if searching for the perfect place to bed down. Dad was suddenly there beside me and we both watched them for a moment. At one point, they all lifted off their branches like a giant black cloud, chattering and screeching and then settled back down in another tree as if they'd all changed their minds as one.

"You're right. I should have brought a gun," said Dad and he started to sing an old nursery rhyme. "Four and twenty blackbirds baked in a pie..." He broke off and looked at me. "No, Adie, I think this place will be good for us."

Sure, I thought. So far it had been *me* who had phoned Mum to let her know we had arrived safely, *me* who had cooked dinner... I could clearly see how it was good for him, but I wasn't so convinced for myself. Dad suddenly shuddered violently.

"Someone's just walked over my grave," he announced and shuddered again.

As the light faded outside, we went through to the lounge, the room with the giant flat-screen in it (which the house still managed to dwarf), and sat on the floral sofa like two bookends, watching a lame chat show on Freeview. When we both felt we'd done our duty by spending enough time in each other's company, we were able to retreat to our separate wings.

"Tomorrow we'll go for a walk and explore this place properly," Dad promised as I drew level with my room. "And *I'll* make you breakfast."

"Yeah, okay, whatever." I figured even *he* couldn't burn cornflakes.

"Night, Ade. Don't let the ghosts keep you awake!"

I went and cleaned my teeth in the spacious bathroom a couple of doors down from my bedroom, looking around in awe as I did so. It was actually more than twice the size of my bedroom back home. There was an old-fashioned toilet – with the high-up cistern – and a very large, free-standing bath (but no shower, I noticed). The taps were gold (or bronze) and there were chequered black and white tiles on the floor, which presumably weren't cheap lino like we had in east London. Next to the basin stood a wooden cabinet on top of which someone, presumably Mrs Dodds (seeing as Jeeves was a product of my father's warped imagination), had laid out towels and individually wrapped soaps, a selection of miniature shower gels and shampoos along with a pumice stone and even a couple of disposable razors. I felt like I was back in a posh hotel from the days when me and Mum would meet up with Dad while he was on tour. I studied my face in the mirror but couldn't find anything to shave except a shadow on my top lip which I had been carefully cultivating for more than a week now.

I looked a little harder at myself. You'd be forgiven for not realising I was Craig Cooper's kid straight off. With different skin tones and different hair we were obviously nothing alike. I had known this for a long time but staring at myself like that, it came starkly back to me: I was spending my summer with a stranger.

Eventually I walked down the creaky corridor and into my room. Everything was dark and unfamiliar, the room thrown into heavy shadows from the dim bedside light. My uncool pyjamas sat there on the four-poster, a token from a life that suddenly seemed impossibly far away. I walked over to the bed, ripping off my t-shirt and kicking away my trainers. Something stirred in the far corner of my room and I spun around. Against a background of fluid brown shadows, a pale shapeless ghost-like figure was rising slowly up from the floor, accompanied by a deep moaning noise.

I don't think I screamed – I really hope I didn't – but I did fall over in my haste to get back to the door, cursing and panting as the shape billowed taller and taller, now the size of a fully grown man, the dim light from my bedside lamp twitching across its blank surface to create grotesque human features. But then, with an incongruous clang inside my panicked brain, I realised that the thing, whatever it was, was laughing at me. I reached for the door knob, still unable to decipher what I was seeing. Dad pulled the sheet from his head.

"Mate, you should see your face!" And he doubled over with laughter.

For a moment I just stood there. I could feel myself trembling but in a flash it had gone from fear to fury.

"Get the hell out of my room!" I hollered and it was all I could do not to thump him as he passed me. I booted shut the door and then, still mad as hell, threw both my trainers at it. They bounced stupidly back off the wood so I kicked them around the room a bit longer, shouting and cursing as I did so. I wanted to punch something but all the furniture was old-fashioned and heavy and I knew I would probably break my knuckles in the process. Besides, the thing I wanted to punch most was Dad. Still panting like an out-of-condition sprinter, I flopped down on the mattress, my hands clutching at my head, hating this house and hating my father even more. I decided first thing in the morning I was calling Mum.

CHAPTER TWELVE

I awoke many hours later, sunshine streaming into my room. I had slept much better than I was expecting and was almost disappointed to find I hadn't tossed and turned all night thanks to my father's childish prank with the dust sheet, which still lay lifelessly in the corner of my room.

I threw on some clothes and went downstairs. Rock music drifted back to me as I came through the first reception room, indicating that my father was already up and attacking the day. The music was suddenly loud enough to form a physical barrier as I opened the heavy kitchen door, taking a step backwards before I could enter.

"What the...?"

"Oh hey kid!" Dad was dancing round the kitchen, banging his head as if he were up on stage. The smell of burnt toast and strong coffee wafted round him. "Breakfast is almost ready!" He punched down the volume on his music system and for a moment I thought I had gone totally deaf. "...cornflakes, Frosties, toast, coffee..." Dad was reeling off his list of accomplishments. "How did you sleep?"

"Good." I reached for the Frosties packet, more forbidden food that you would never find in my mother's kitchen cupboards.

I found myself reading the ingredients (and hating myself for doing so). Dad watched me, smiling slightly. He knows what Mum is like. I pretended not to notice.

More than anything, I wanted to stay mad at him but he was clearly in such a good mood it hardly seemed worth the effort. He poured me a big mug of black coffee and slid it across the counter, cowboy style.

"You drink coffee, right?"

I shook my head.

"Oh." He looked genuinely surprised.

"I'll just grab some OJ."

"Ok. Yeah. Good idea." He watched me go over to the spaceship refrigerator. "Let's take everything through to the dining room and we can eat in there. I could get used to this Lord of the Manor malarkey."

Once again we found ourselves at either ends of the long polished table, staring at one another in the distance as we ate cereal and burnt toast, quietly, (alone but together) in John Parker's magnificent, yet somehow other-worldly, house. The summer was turning out to be slightly surreal, like everything connected with my father, and I sighed.

"You fancy going to explore after this?" Dad called down to me. I shrugged back. "There's some bicycles John said, if you want to go for a ride with your old man?"

"Sure." The last time I had been on a push-bike I must have been about ten. I muttered something about not being very good but couldn't be sure whether Dad would have heard me all the way up at his end of the table.

In LA, Dad had ridden a Harley and I remember him taking me on the back when we came to visit. Mum had been furious when she found out, though she'd done her share of pillion rides with him before I came along so she couldn't really say much except that I was too small.

After breakfast we left the dirty dishes in the sink and went to find those bicycles. Beyond the conservatory was the neatly trimmed lawn, walled on two sides by tall oak trees in which the crows had their nests. A paved path led down to what looked like an oversized shed at the very bottom. It had decking out front and big windows, which cast back a strange metallic reflection of the sky so that you couldn't see inside.

"It's what they call a summer house," said Dad trying the door handle.

"Of course it is. I mean, as if the winter house isn't big enough, right?" I muttered.

Dad smiled. "It's just a glorified shed to the likes of you and me." The door was locked so he peered through the window, hands cupped on either side of his face to block out the harsh glare of the sun. "Man, it's huge in there. It'd make a great studio. Pity we can't get inside."

"There are a load of keys hanging up in the kitchen," I said. "Maybe one of them opens it up."

"We'll try later, shall we? John didn't say anywhere was out of bounds."

"Would it matter to you if he had?"

Dad stepped off the decking and we looked to the edge of the lawn that wasn't screened by trees. "You can see for absolutely miles and miles in this place, can't you?"

"Shame there's chuff-all out there," I shrugged and he laughed.

I turned round then, a distinct feeling that we were being watched. A crow cawed somewhere in the distance behind the shed and a light breeze rippled the branches of the oaks.

"Come on." Dad started to head over to the far side of the lawn where some old outbuildings marked the edge of the tended gardens from the wilder open fields beyond. "Let's go and find John's bicycles."

The stone barns may once have held grain or perhaps been used for animals but were now derelict. We forced open the rusty door handle to the first one we came to, peering into the darkness. It smelled of damp hay. A bird flapped its wings above us and flew off through a hole in the roof bringing down a shower of grit in front of our eyes. We stood there, blinking back the darkness. The only light came from the shaft of sunshine through the broken roof.

Slowly my eyes grew accustomed to the shadows. On the stone walls hung various gardening tools: a spade and a pick-axe, a rusty chainsaw, a hoe with long finger-like prongs, a looped length of heavy chain and a couple of long-handled scythes.

"This must be the torture chamber," hissed Dad in his best horror-film whisper. He gave the chain a swat with his hand and took a couple of steps further inside. The chain creaked as it swung slowly back into position and I shivered. "There. Now someone's walked over your grave too."

Against the far wall we could just make out the dark shapes of a couple of bicycles.

"Bingo!" Dad picked his way over the damp earthy ground but I stayed where I was, in the doorway, feeling the sun reassuringly warm on my back. I don't know why but something made me reluctant to venture any further inside.

The barn air was cold and still against my cheeks and for a moment I thought I could see my breath hanging white and misty in front of my face. But of course that was just my imagination working overtime as usual. Dad took hold of the two bikes.

"Well, come on then," he called waiting for me but still my legs wouldn't move. He paused then shunted one of the bicycles towards me. I watched it wobble in my direction then fall onto its side with a soft clatter against the middle of the dirt floor. "That one's definitely yours. Doesn't know where it's going either."

Dad wheeled his towards the door and I had to move out of the way to let him pass.

"Go and get your bike then," he said rolling his out into the sunshine to inspect it and reluctantly I stepped a little further into the dank shed.

The bicycle lay on its side on the musty packed-earth floor, a shaft of sunlight glinting off its frame. I reached gingerly down to pick it up but as I took hold of the handlebar a cold, damp hand slid wetly over mine, icy fingers intertwined with my own. I recoiled violently, falling back onto my arse, my feet slipping desperately over the dusty ground as I tried to get up again. I scrabbled backwards but in that same instant the shed door swung closed behind me and for a moment the barn was plunged into complete blackness, with me trapped inside. I screamed and Dad pushed open the door again letting the sunlight back in.

"What did you do that for?" I barrelled into him as I forced my way out into the sunshine.

"Do what? I didn't do anything!"

We stood there, looking accusingly at one another.

"There's something in there!" I told him eventually.

Dad just laughed. He looked ridiculous holding that push-bike. "Have you been on the sauce this morning?"

"I swear down! Something touched my hand!"

Dad looked at me, then cursed. "Here." He thrust his bicycle towards me and went back inside the barn. A moment later he reappeared with the other bike, still cursing. But he was laughing at me too: his prank last night had me proper spooked, which was probably exactly what he wanted.

"I'm telling you," I mumbled, gripping the bicycle handlebars in my sweaty palms, "something touched my hand."

"You always did have an overactive imagination." I watched him swing his leg over the little bike. He looked like a giant child or a performing bear. A moment later he was wobbling off down the path, laughing and swearing, long blond hair flying out behind him, a clown in his own bizarre circus. "Well come on then"!" he shouted after me. "Don't let the bogey man get you!"

CHAPTER THIRTEEN

We met Mrs Dodds the following morning. She pulled up in an old Fiat 500 and let herself in through the back door as we were having breakfast in the dining room.

"I see you've made yourselves at home," she mumbled no doubt referring to the stack of dirty pans left soaking in the sink from the night before.

Dad had insisted we leave them to soak overnight so that they would be easier to clean. The smell of stale curry clung to the kitchen walls this morning, the ghost of last night's dinner.

"Mrs Dodds, I presume," said Dad.

Mrs Dodds nodded. "And you must be that rock star Mr Parker was telling me about."

"Guilty as charged," grinned Dad. "Voodoo Mary."

"Mary?" Mrs Dodds looked confused. "What kind of name is that for a grown man?"

Dad frowned. "No, that's the name of the band. Voodoo Mary. You're not a fan, I take it?"

She looked around the room. "I don't bother myself much with rock music," she commented as if it was something distasteful to her. "I see the power was out last night?" She nodded to the candle stubs melted onto saucers and plates standing on the sideboard. I suppose we could have been having a romantic candle-lit meal, but she was right. It had been out for about two hours. Luckily my iPad had a full charge and I'd just finished cooking. "You want to be careful with those candles, mind. You know a blaze took out most of the upstairs a hundred or so years back? If it's happened once, it can happen again. Houses are funny like that."

"Hilarious. But we'll be careful, scouts honour," promised Dad, clumsily doing something with his fingers to simulate a scout sign.

I secretly willed Mrs Dodds to get on with her cleaning before the fingers morphed into something less appropriate. He can be more of a kid than I am sometimes. She was looking at *me* now, and I found myself sitting more upright in my chair, taking my elbows off the table. My mum gets that look sometimes too so I know what it means.

"This is my son, Adie," said Dad and I waited as she looked me up and down, the frown lines growing deeper on her forehead.

I wondered if she was going to say how we didn't look alike and I braced slightly.

"Nice to meet you," she nodded finally and I relaxed again. "I'll start upstairs, then."

Dad watched her grab the plastic holder of cleaning products. "You might wanna leave my bathroom for a while," he muttered quietly. "That curry last night..." He turned back to me. "What were you trying to do, Adie? Kill your old man?"

I just stared into my cornflakes and said nothing.

Before she left, Mrs Dodds scrubbed the pans in the sink, much to my annoyance, leaving them gleaming on the draining board.

"Make me a list of any food you need and you can ring it through to me Tuesday or Wednesday," she said briskly. "My number's on the pad by the phone."

"I thought Tesco delivers?" I frowned and she gave a tight little laugh.

"Not up here. No chance. No one comes up here. You're lucky Mr Parker pays so well else you wouldn't see me for dust neither." She folded up the flowery overall she had been wearing and stuffed it into her voluminous handbag. "No, you tell me what you want and I'll order it for you. They'll come out as far as Lower Huffingham but that's it. I'll bring your shopping with me next time I come up here."

"But what if we run out of something in the meantime?" asked Dad incredulously.

Mrs Dodds fixed him with her rodent eyes and he shot me a naughty-schoolboy kind of look.

"I suppose you'll just have to do without. Like normal folk, Mr Rock-Star Music-Man," she mumbled, half to herself.

I bit my lip trying not to smile.

"I guess she won't be asking for my autograph, then," muttered Dad as she turned towards the kitchen door.

Once she had gone, we spent the afternoon playing on Dad's Xbox as the sky clouded over outside and large pellets of summer rain splattered against the tall windows, the house mottled with metallic shadows. Time slipped away and before I knew it, another day had passed us by. I looked hungrily at Dad.

"Tomorrow, Adie, I promise. Tomorrow I'll organise us something really special."

I waited but he wouldn't look me in the eye now, packing away the games console and reaching for the remote control.

"Fine." I stomped off to the kitchen to see what I could make into a meal, hearing the TV click on behind me as Dad let out a contented sigh.

The next morning he said he was going to do some work so I left him in John's spacious office where he'd set up all his music equipment – the far room on what we'd taken to calling the East Wing. I grabbed the big bunch of keys off the wall in the kitchen and went to explore by myself.

I crossed the lawn with this old set of rusting keys heavy in my hand and walked over to the summer house by the far trees, pausing for a moment as I watched the reflection of the clouds skating over its silvery windows. The crows eyed me warily from their treetop perches as I stepped onto the decking and started to jiggle various keys in the lock. I was onto the fifth key before I felt it turn and for whatever reason my heart quickened suddenly at the prospect of going inside.

I pushed open the door and stood on the threshold for a moment, breathing in the smell of the wood and the stale warm air. What happened yesterday with the bicycles came back to me and I lingered a moment longer before I could force myself to step inside.

Unlike the other shed, this was a well-equipped, comfortable living space complete with armchairs and a small table along with cupboards and even a sink. It could have been a self-contained granny flat and instantly I wished Nana Sara could be here with me. I found a light switch and flicked it on.

"Hello?" For some reason I felt the need to announce myself and I paused, half-expecting a reply.

I edged further into the room. Someone had previously used it as an artist's studio and I could now distinctly smell the dried-up paint and a faint tang of turps. In the far corner were a couple of easels, covered with the white sheeting that seemed to cover everything in this unloved, un-lived-in house. I tugged at the corner of one of the sheets, and it fell away to reveal a woman's dark-skinned face staring back at me. She looked very pretty though the picture was unfinished: the background was blank and her neck and shoulders were sketched in outline only. I stared at it for a while, letting the sheeting fall in a soft heap at my feet as I wondered who she might be.

On the next easel was a picture of John Parker's house, painted in oils, standing against a sky of soft pinky-purpley clouds not dissimilar to the sky I had seen on our first night here. It was odd to look at it there, captured so clearly in oils, almost as if I was having an out-of-body experience, staring at myself staring at the house.

Whoever had painted these pictures clearly had talent and I peered into the corner of the landscape trying to read the signature. It looked like *G W* and had been dated 1908. I checked that again, surprised that a painting, which was over one-hundred years old, should have been left here, as though someone still intended to come back to it after all this time. Maybe they planned to add to it or paint over the canvas with something new. As I bent into the picture I got that feeling again, as if someone was watching me, and I spun round, half expecting to see my father standing there, or Phil the gardener, but as my eyes darted warily about the summer house I realised, of course, I was completely alone.

I ate lunch by myself in the kitchen. Dad said the muse had hit him and he didn't want to break his concentration so I left him there, a guitar on his knee, laptop on the desk beside him, a pencil in his mouth and scraps of paper all over the floor. Genius takes many forms, I suppose, but I couldn't help wondering whether this was just going to be his excuse for not cooking dinner again tonight. I stewed on that as I ate my sandwich, plugged into Swedish House Mafia as a distraction from Dad's music.

Afterwards I took a mooch around the house determined not to think about the lack of dinner, which I convinced myself was now a foregone conclusion. In the room next to Dad's makeshift music studio was a library with floor to ceiling shelves, many of which held worn leather-bound books, giving it that proper old library feel. I wondered if John Parker had bought these in a charity shop, or at a house clearance, to add to the authentic feel of the place, or whether they too, like much of the furniture, had been passed down to each new owner of the property. I found a copy of Mark Twain's *Adventures of Huckleberry Finn* and settled into one of the armchairs to lose myself for a few hours, turning up the volume on Robert Johnson's *Dead Shrimp Blues* so as to set the mood and blot out the electric guitar periodically twanging from the adjoining room.

When I next looked up it was almost four o'clock. Books have always been able to do that to me. And I've been reading even more just lately, since the voices began. I find that stuffing my ears with music and my head with words works well at blocking out those unwanted interruptions.

Presently I tugged a single white earbud from one ear and re-grounded myself in the here and now. The music next door appeared to have stopped but there were no obvious signs of dinner being cooked. I absolutely refused to go and remind him. I almost wanted him to forget so that I could hate him even more for his total lack of parental concern. Mum had made me promise to give it to the end of the week before I finalised my decision about coming home.

Dad was on the phone in John's office. I listened for a moment before re-stuffing my ears with blues and sliding the volume back up. I bent open the musty pages of my book again and set sail down the Mississippi with Huck and Jim as another couple of hours fell away.

By now it was half-past six and I figured it was safe to say something because it was obvious that Dad had completely neglected his fatherly responsibilities of feeding me and therefore I could feel duly aggrieved. I put down Mark Twain and went next door. Dad was frowning hard into a sheet of scribbled lyrics. He looked up suddenly as I came through.

"Oh, hey son," he smiled like nothing was wrong. He took the pencil out of his mouth and held it over the paper. "You're good with words. What rhymes with metal?"

I scowled at him. "Dinner?"

He frowned some more, as if he was considering this to be my answer. "Your eyes as cold as metal, but your skin as soft as dinner? No, Adie, that just doesn't work for me."

"What's for dinner?" I demanded, refusing to be drawn in by his easy laughter.

"Hungry are you?" He jotted down something that obviously rhymed better than my suggestion then read it back to himself in his head. "Don't worry, your old man has taken care of everything just as he promised."

"You have?" I felt almost cheated.

"Said I would, didn't I?" He shrugged as if he had never forgotten anything in his life and then went back to his lyrics. "Give it another forty minutes. Think you can possibly hang on that long?"

I mumbled something and went off to the kitchen to find signs of this mysterious dinner of his. There was nothing in the oven. No vegetables had been chopped up in anticipation. Nothing from the freezer was thawing on the side. I opened the microwave but that was empty too. Then I just sat there, Beethoven blaring in my ears, my head on my arms, waiting, waiting for him to admit he had cocked up. Mum would have to let me come home then.

I read once that Beethoven had a difficult relationship with his father too.

Dad came through at half past seven and grabbed some plates and cutlery. I watched him, wondering if he even realised there was still no food to put on those plates.

"Shouldn't be long now," he said and went through to the dining room.

I followed him as he set out our usual two places. By now he was starting to scare me. I mean, I knew he had done a lot of drugs when he was younger and they had affected him in all kinds of ways but this? This was why I always needed to be able to contact the outside world. At that moment, a bell sounded in the kitchen followed by a thumping on the front door.

"That must be the doorbell," said Dad. "Didn't even think those old bells still worked."

I followed him out to the hall. I could see through the window that a black cab was now sitting on the forecourt.

"Are we going out for dinner?" I asked as he pulled open the front door, a big grin on his face.

"Al'right Guv'nor," said the driver. "So this is where you're hiding, is it?"

"Nice one Kev." Dad took the large polystyrene box that the driver offered him. "You want to come in for a bit before you head off?"

The driver shook his head. "Naa, don't want to be caught on these country roads after dark. I'd never find my way back to civilisation."

"Tell me about it." Dad gave me the box to hold. It was ever so slightly warm and smelled faintly of food despite the lid wedged into the top. He'd got us a takeaway? I watched him peel a fifty off a roll of notes from his jeans pocket and hand it over to 'Kev'. "That's for your trouble. The rest still goes on the account, I assume? Beck will clear it at the end of the month I guess."

"Yeah no worries." Kevin pocketed the fifty-pound note, waving once as he climbed back into his vehicle. I stared in amazement as the rounded outline of the London black cab disappeared down the long flat drive and out of sight.

"You bought us a takeaway?" I frowned as Dad shut the door again.

"Not just *any* takeaway. The best Thai in London." He lifted the lid with a squeak.

I looked at the numerous cartons nestled inside this polystyrene hamper I was still holding. "You had a takeaway delivered all the way from London?"

"You like Thai, don't you?" Dad took the box from me. "We might need to warm it up a bit, mind. God, that smells good!"

"You got a taxi to bring a takeaway all the way from London? To here?" I repeated, unable to fathom what he had just done. "But, but how much did that cost?"

I don't think I was even that bothered about the money, I just didn't have the words to express my utter disbelief. My father simply laughed.

"Since when did you have to worry about money? You want me to nuke this for you or you think we can make do as is?" He was already sitting down at the top of the dining table, pulling out various plastic containers and paper cartons. He looked up at me, misreading the dumb-founded expression on my face. "Your mum cooks Thai, doesn't she? I thought you'd like it. They even opened the kitchen two hours early for us to get this here on time."

I sank down into my chair at the other end of the table, just staring at him as he continued to open up the numerous cartons, releasing the faintest of tangy aromas into the cavernous room. "So what was all that stuff about fresh food and cooking everything from scratch?" I demanded.

"It's just one takeaway, Adie. What's the big deal?"

He looked at me and I was finally forced to come over to his end of the table. I gazed at the fine feast now spread out in ten or so little containers and paper bags. Yeah. I like Thai food. I snatched at one of the cartons. Yeah. Dad had sorted out dinner. I reached for another container then whisked the food back to my seat at the far end of the table, a squirrel with its winter nuts. Dad had done as he had promised. He had fixed dinner. So why was I feeling the way that I was?

CHAPTER FOURTEEN

That night I listened to the wind blowing through the branches of the trees, imagined all those crows being tossed around this way and that as they clung to their beds, waiting for it to calm down so they could shut their dark, glassy eyes and rest. And like them, I also refused to let sleep come.

I ran through the conversation that I would have with Mum the next morning. I couldn't work out how best to phrase what had happened for maximum impact. I knew that sending for a takeaway was cheating on his part, and it would piss Mum off if she thought we were living on nothing but junk food again, but I didn't know how to convey this to her without sounding like a snivelling brat who was simply telling tales on his father.

So far I had cooked every dinner – barring the one takeaway; I had been spooked and humiliated by Dad's practical joke with the dust sheet, had this weird feeling that someone was watching me the whole time and had distinctly felt *something* touch my hand in the bicycle shed that day. Oh, and just so you know, Dad had crashed into me later that same afternoon when he fell off his bike. Being my father, of course, he didn't just lose his balance and fall off. That would be far too normal. Instead, he claimed it was due to the pendant he wore round his neck suddenly burning onto his chest as it warmed in the sun. And he says I have an overactive imagination? All I had was a big gash on my knee from our collision.

No, I still needed more ammunition, one more mega Dad-sized cock-up to warrant Mum sending John

Parker to bring me home again. I didn't have to wait long.

Dad's PA, Becky Frazer, came out to see us after we had been in John's house for a week. She turned up on the doorstep Saturday morning all glossy smiles and sunglasses, air kissing me as she strode confidently into the hall amidst a choking cloud of perfume. When I didn't react, she wheeled round and looked at me, pushing her sunglasses up into her sleek red hair.

"I'm sorry, did your hamster just die or something?"

Dad guffawed, making a comment about me sulking because I was being forced to spend time in his company rather than hanging round with my 'little chums' back home. Not that Dad even knew the name of any one of my so-called 'little chums'.

"You're chatting shit, man," I scowled, which just made him laugh harder.

"Least you're not breaking into cars, eh Adie?" he shouted as I stomped off to the library to lose myself in another old book. "Or tagging walls, or whatever it is you young people get up to." And I heard him chuckling to himself as he led the lovely Becky into the kitchen to make her something to drink. It irritated me that he should try and play the dutiful parent for her when he was so woefully inadequate for the task.

I looked over the leathery spines on the library shelves, wondering which one to escape into for the morning when I got that feeling again – as though someone was watching me – and, as I turned, this time I glimpsed an old man standing out the front of the house, just staring in through the long library windows. On seeing me, he pulled away from the glass then walked slowly off round the side of the house.

Once upon a time when something like that happened you could bet it was a fan, some crazy stalker of Voodoo Mary, but this guy didn't exactly look like a Heavy Metal aficionado. One time, a woman stuffed a pair of knickers through our letterbox whilst loudly declaring her undying love for my father until Mum called the police on her. Like I said, my early life was a bit of a freak-show and my dad was King Freak.

I walked back through the length of the great house turning the corner at the far end into the kitchen where Becky and Dad were bent over the table, signing papers.

"There's somebody in the garden," I announced, trying not to sound spooked again.

"Yeah?" Dad glanced unconcernedly out of the windows. "It's probably Phil, the gardener. He comes at the weekends apparently."

"Lucky him," sniggered Becky, and Dad snorted a laugh too and then for some reason they both looked at me. I could feel my face growing hot.

"I'll go and check it's not some crazed psycho stalker, shall I?" I muttered and went for the back door.

"He's a good kid really," I heard Dad tell Becky as I let myself out.

I wondered what the hell he would know about it.

At the far edge of the lawn I could see the door to one of the outbuildings was open so I walked towards it, slowing as I got nearer, and then just standing a little way away, unwilling to go inside again in case the monster, whatever it was, was still in there. Presently the man I had glimpsed earlier backed out of the doorway with one of the long-handled scythes in his arms and as he turned, catching sight of me, he jumped, grabbing a fistful of his plaid shirt as if he were having a heart-attack.

"Hey, what are you doing creeping around like that?" he demanded when he had recovered himself enough to be angry with me. "You don't want to sneak up on people when they're carrying this in their arms." He swung the scythe down to the ground. "Lose your head before you know it."

"I'm not sneaking," I shrugged. "And what are you doing spying on people?"

"Didn't know anyone was in," he muttered, walking past me with the scythe now cradled protectively against his chest. He cast me a nasty sideways glance. "You must be that musician's boy."

I watched him walk away. "Yeah." How many times had I heard that? My father will always define me. I followed after him. "And you must be the gardener. Unless you're some demented scythe killer?"

He stopped and turned back to me, frowning hard. "That supposed to be funny?"

I shrugged and he walked on. After a while I followed him. He walked for some time, along the far edge of the property as if he were looking for something. Eventually he stopped to one side of the house where unkempt brambles blocked his path. He turned round, as if surprised to find I was still there, then took a giant swing and cut a swathe out of the brambles, then another: swish, swoosh. I watched him.

"Wouldn't a chainsaw be quicker?" I shouted as he kept on arcing the ancient scythe through the gnarly bushes.

Eventually he stopped. "Maybe." He wiped a hand over his forehead then took another angry swing with his weapon. "But this gets the blood pumping better." He swung the scythe a couple more times, cutting a hole into the thick sprawl of brambles, then paused again to look back at me. "Mind you, if I wanted to kill someone I'd choose a chainsaw over a scythe any day."

"What?" I thought I'd misheard him.

"Didn't you call me a demented killer back there?"

"Yeah, well I just meant…" But he'd started cutting again by now – a slow rhythmic motion – once to the left and once to the right; left, right; like a swashbuckling pirate. "Unless you actually are…" I added.

"I could be for all you know," he panted. "Perfect place for a demented killer is this, I'm sure. No one to hear you scream!"

"Yeah, I'm shaking here." If he wanted me to be scared, he was out of luck.

"Well, you must have heard the stories about this place," he shouted back, still cutting, angling his words over his shoulder to me.

"Not really."

He paused then, eyebrows raised in delight. "No? Mmm. Fancy that. Well, what d'you think of it so far?"

I shrugged my shoulders wondering where to start. "Bit boring. There's not a lot to do out here, is there?"

"Aye, I suppose not; not for a young person like yourself, anyway." He looked me up and down as he considered my comments. "And what about your father? What does he think of the place?"

I shrugged again, wanting to make some flippant comment to lighten the conversation. "My dad's pretty easy going. He likes anywhere so long as there's a well-stocked booze cabinet for him." But as soon as I'd said it I felt guilty because I knew there was no booze in the house. That was why we were both here, stuck out in the middle of nowhere, in the first place.

Phil the gardener digested this, taking it to be serious rather than the joke I had half-intended. He shook his head. "Well the man's an idiot then." And he went back to his cutting leaving me with an inexplicable desire to defend my father.

"So what do they say about this place?" I called after a while, uncomfortable with the lingering subject of my father's shortcomings.

"You really don't know?" Phil stopped and looked at me. "Don't you feel it? Feel it in the walls of the house? Something of unimaginable evil they tell me."

I wasn't expecting that. John Parker's words from when we first arrived came back to me, the stuff about the gargoyles being there to ward off evil spirits. Maybe he knew more than he had let on.

"Who says that?"

"People. People that have stayed up there in the house," he nodded back.

"It's an old house," I shrugged. "People like telling spooky stories."

"Yeah but no one's been able to make a home in it for nigh on a hundred years now," called Phil bending down and swooshing through the brambles again. "Not since the great fire. Plenty have tried, mind. Had more owners over the last century than I've had hot dinners."

"That doesn't prove anything," I said.

"Doesn't it?" He looked over his shoulder at me.

I shrugged. "I don't know. You tell me."

"Not for me to say," said Phil in such a way that you knew this was exactly what he was about to do. "The Oakley family lived here till around the late eighteen-hundreds. Local family. Good people. Then it was the Wetherbys who took up residence and not long after that came the fire. You've heard about the fire I take it?"

I nodded and he seemed a little disappointed. He swung the scythe back through the brambles.

"Swept through the upstairs it did, destroying most of the front of the house and taking the life of their eldest son in the process," he continued. "Suppose that might have had something to do with it. By all accounts the fire marked the beginning of the end for this old house, and after the Wetherby family died off no one has settled here since. No one at all. House is like a prison, they all claim, like the walls are closing in on you. Fancy that, huh?" He stopped and laughed at me. "Some even say they've seen the ghost of John Wetherby himself roaming restlessly through the grounds, driven mad by the death of his son." He stopped and looked hard at me, checking that his words were having the desired effect. I twitched my shoulders, exhaled to make clear that they weren't.

"The landlord of the Green Man is the person you want to talk to about these things if you're interested. He knows more about it than I do but I'll stake my life on there being *something* behind all the stories, no smoke without fire as the saying goes." He laughed to himself. "If you'll pardon the pun."

I watched as he swung the scythe back through the bushes. Had what happened to me in the shed just been a figment of my imagination, or was there really something malevolent living alongside us as Phil would have me believe? I turned to go when Phil straightened back up.

"Daresay you'll be able to tell me if they're right, eh? If you and your dad last the summer, that is." And his mouth curled into a victorious sneer.

I left him to his ghostly ramblings and swashbuckling scything and went back across the lawn towards the kitchen. Becky was just collecting up her things as I came in.

"Well it's good to see you both looking so healthy," she said, flashing me her LA smile of perfect white teeth. "The country air is obviously agreeing with you."

I slumped into a seat at the table as they both got up.

"Oh, and I mustn't forget this or Stu will never forgive me." She bent down and pulled out a DVD box set from her bag. "He was most insistent I give you this. Said you wouldn't have anything worth watching otherwise."

Dad looked puzzled, but shrugged easily. "We used to watch this on tour. Mind you we were usually high as kites at the time." He took the box set and walked Becky to her car leaving me to chew on a thumbnail and worry quietly about what Phil had told me.

I came through to the living room just as Dad was closing up one of the cases of the DVDs. He looked up, guiltily. "Hey kid, what d'you fancy for lunch?"

I shrugged, not even that hungry yet. "What's the box set?"

"Oh, just a comedy we used to watch. Don't know if it's your thing exactly. Stu's got weird taste in this kind of stuff. I'll just go and put it in my room and then we'll make lunch."

I watched him walk up the stairs wondering whether it could have been a porno or something. Why else would he be acting all furtive like that? And why put it in his room when the DVD player was downstairs? I felt like telling him there would be nothing on it that I hadn't already seen on the internet but he didn't give me the chance. Probably he still thought of me as a little kid. I wondered if he even knew when my birthday was. It was probably Becky who kept him on track with all that kind of stuff and just thinking about her gave me a little ripple under my skin.

Maybe it was my imagination but Dad seemed to be acting weird for the rest of the day. In fact he went to bed really early, claiming to be tired, leaving me downstairs watching a programme on gangsters. Eventually I switched it off and went upstairs too, uncomfortable at being left on my own in that big empty room. I walked to my bedroom but then something inexplicably made me keep on walking and I turned the corner at the end of the corridor and tiptoed along the East Wing towards my father's room. Maybe I just intended to listen at his door, to satisfy my own curiosity about the DVD, thinking that he might be watching it on his laptop or something. Even though the last thing I wanted to see was my father sitting alone in his bedroom watching porn, I couldn't stop myself from heading over there.

My feet slowed as I got to his door. At the bottom I could see a bright strip of light, way too bright for just ordinary lighting and I found myself anxiously pushing open his door. Several things went through my brain just then, all jostling to be registered first. I noticed that my father wasn't watching porn. In fact he wasn't watching anything. He was sprawled unconscious on top of his bed, spread-eagled over the covers. I instantly recognised the unmistakable smell of dope too, and clocked the burnt-down stub of a joint between his fingers. Oh, and also, his curtains were on fire. Somehow he must have set fire to them with the joint.

"Dad!" I tugged desperately at one foot but he was a dead weight, completely out of his skull.

The brightness from the flaming curtains was suddenly blinding. I knew I had to put that out before the smoke got too much, although at the time all I was aware of was the intense brightness of the flames – no heat, no smoke – just a brilliant yellow light with three-foot high flames licking dangerously up the drapes beside his bed.

In a panic, I raced to his bathroom next door in search of something I could fill up with water. On the floor was a white plastic bin, which I threw under the bath tap, furiously opening the bronze tap-head as far as it would go to fill the plastic bin with cold water. Whatever else I thought about my deadbeat Dad, I instantly knew that I didn't want him to die. Then I rushed back to his bedroom.

He was still lying motionless on the bed but this time the curtains were definitely *not* on fire. Thoughts raced, nonsensical, inside my head. Unfortunately though I was on automatic, the bin already drawn back under one arm. As I realised that his bedroom was not actually burning to the ground, my brain had already instructed my arm to chuck the bucket of water. Everything seemed to slow down. I was aware of myself hurling cold water across Dad's bed to put out the now non-existent fire and as I released the sluice of water, I think I shouted something, some stupid garbled warning to my father.

Moments later, he bolted upright, spluttering, wide-eyed, gasping and dripping wet and we just stared at each other as if neither of us could believe what had just happened. My mouth was open but I couldn't get any words out. Dad looked about him, then down at the drenched stub of joint still between his fingers, then back to me with an empty plastic bin in my hands.

"Adie," he started but I backed away a couple of steps. "Mate, Adie, I'm sorry." He lumbered off the bed towards me but I turned and fled, dropping the bin as I ran. "Adie, please! I didn't mean to."

I raced to my room and flung shut the door. My chest heaved painfully in the darkness. I could hear him plodding down the corridor towards me and then he was the other side of the wood, tapping gently against it with one of his big silver skull rings.

"Mate, please, let's just talk about this."

He thought I'd chucked a bucket of water on him because I'd caught him sneaking a joint in his room. I slid down to the floor, my heart thudding against my rib cage, listening to him plead sorrowfully on the other side of the door. In my mind I could still see the yellow flames devouring his curtains, felt again the adrenaline kicking in, the sudden absolute certainty that I did not want him to die. Then I could see those same curtains, hanging quietly, my father prone and snoring on his bed. I held my head in my hands as tightly as I possibly could.

"Adie, please, talk to me," wailed Dad.

But how could I tell him I was losing my mind? I buried my head in my arms, my knees scrunched up against my chest, shutting my eyes as they grew hot and blurry. Eventually my father gave up and walked slowly back to his room.

CHAPTER FIFTEEN

We ate breakfast the next morning in the kitchen, moving round one another without talking, being careful not to get in each other's way, communicating with the absolute minimum of words. It was Sunday and I had been here with him for over a week. I had served my time. Eventually Dad let out a long, heavy sigh and looked at me.

"Adie, mate, son, I'm so very sorry about last night."

I kept looking down into my cereal bowl, dragging the spoon round and round as everything grew soggy in its sea of milk.

"Give me a guitar and I can do anything you like," Dad said. "No question. But give me my son to look after and I screw up. I always do." He shook his head, looked around the kitchen. I could see him in the corner of my vision even though I was refusing to make eye contact. "You know, I didn't plan it. Stu slipped something in with those DVDs he gave Becky. And I know that's no excuse, but I guess he knows what I'm like: will power of a kitten, right? Mind you, he just thinks it's all a big laugh." He looked directly at me now, frowning hard. "But it's not, is it?"

I felt my shoulders lift involuntarily through my t-shirt. He paused. The motor at the back of the fridge started to whir. A crow cawed outside on the lawn.

"So I suppose you're going to call your mum now, let her know?"

I glanced up suspiciously. "Why?"

Dad sighed again and put his head in his hands, long blond hair falling between his ringed fingers "I know you called her before, Adie, after my sheet-stunt. I'm sorry but I really didn't think that would upset you as much as it did."

"It didn't," I snapped. A lie and he probably knew it, but what else could I say?

"You still wanted to go home, though, didn't you? Even back on our first night. Not that I blame you. I mean, who'd want to be stuck all the way out here with me, eh?" And he grunted out a single, sad laugh. "It was your mum's idea really. She's worried about you, Adie. She thought it might be good for you to get away from everything in London for a while, but then again, she didn't factor in me, did she, cocking up all her carefully laid plans? No. Call her. If you want to go home, then I won't stop you."

We both sat across the big wooden table from one another. I felt bad for chucking water on him and letting him think it was because I was so disgusted with him, or for calling Mum and telling tales, begging to come home. He was right. I'd been determined to hate every minute of it, right from the start, willing him to fail and now that he had I suddenly felt like it was *me* that had let *him* down. I quickly pushed those feelings away.

"Fine. If that's what you want, then I'll go," I mumbled with another quick jerk of my shoulders, letting him know that I wasn't bothered either way.

I wanted to be angry with him because that was so much easier than anything else.

"Of course it's not what I want," said Dad. "But I also know that I'm not exactly Father of the Year material."

I snorted. "Yeah, you ain't lying." And I realised I'd managed it. From the pit of my stomach I had dredged up a familiar churning swamp of anger and

Dad was standing there with a big old target on his back as usual.

"Maybe I should take parenting classes, what d'you think?"

"Don't waste your money. You'd only flunk it."

Dad took it all, soaking up my anger like a sponge. That's one thing I'll say for him: he puts his hands up when he's wrong. "It's a lot easier being a rock star than being a dad, Adie, let me tell you."

"Just as well," I mumbled. At least Dad had always provided for us financially. I had travelled halfway across the world thanks to Voodoo Mary; stayed in some of the poshest hotels; had an iPad and a laptop and a PC; had the money to blow my future a hundred times over if I chose to. "Least you've got a fall-back."

"Yeah well, in the music biz you've got a whole load of people doing stuff for you, catching you when you fall, when you screw up," Dad told me, "but being a parent, now that's one tough gig. And you've got to do it all on your own." He exhaled, ran his hands through his hair. "Mind you, your mum's always done it on her own, hasn't she? And she's done a great job. Guess it's just me. Maybe I'm not cut out to be a father."

"Well gee," I snarled, "sorry for being such a giant inconvenience to you then."

The anger, far from the bile it really was, tasted like caramel in my throat.

"God, Adie, you've got nothing to be sorry for," my father exclaimed. "You were the best thing I ever put my name to, better than any number-one song, any tune I ever wrote, anything. It's me that's sorry. You deserve so much better."

He got up and poured himself another mug of coffee. I realised with a slight panic that he was going to send me home now because he thought that's what he *should* do, the only option left to him, my dad the screw-up, and I also realised – in that same split second – that I didn't actually want to go. He stared out over the lawns towards the summer house. The back of his t-shirt listed last autumn's tour dates for a band that had once supported Voodoo Mary, now headliners in their own right. Dad had got us tickets to their gig but then hadn't turned up for the show so I'd gone to see them on my own. I never told Mum.

I looked at him in his black jeans and boots, band t-shirt, silver rings and tattoos. How many people out there in the world would give their right arm to sit where I was, having breakfast with Voodoo Mary front man, Craig Cooper, I wondered? He turned back from the window.

"You've got every right to be angry with me. I know that."

I looked away, feeling guilty now.

"I screwed up again. I know that too."

Perhaps I should have just told him the truth about my hallucinations. I scratched at my arms, dug my thumbnail into the soft wood of the old kitchen table as Dad cleared his throat awkwardly.

"And I certainly know that I've got no right to ask anything of you, Adie, but if you'd just give me one more chance, I promise I will try my absolute damndest not to screw things up between us."

I took a long while to reply, not wanting to believe him but having no choice; the same old, same old.

"You're just scared of what Mum's gonna say," I mumbled finally when I thought he had sweated enough.

Dad laughed, a giant laugh of relief, then swore, then apologised for swearing. "Too right. And your grandma Sara. Man, she is one scary broad when she wants to be."

I desperately wanted to stay angry with him but it was too late: it had already fizzled out. I suddenly remembered being very little and Dad giving me a hug after I had fallen over and grazed my hand, a brief split second when he wasn't Dad the Rock Star but Dad the Dad.

He flinched suddenly.

"Shit, what the…?" He was fumbling with the neck of his t-shirt pulling out the necklace he always wore: a deep green gem stone that had been threaded onto a thin loop of black leather. He held it out in front of him awkwardly. "It's hot. It's burning hot again!"

I let go of the breath I was holding. The circus had rolled back into town and the moment was lost, as always. He looked at my face.

"No really, Adie. It's red hot. Feel it." He leaned over to me holding the pendant out for me to touch.

"Really, Dad, whatever, I believe you," I lied, turning away.

"I mean it." He was fumbling with the catch at the back of his neck and eventually he dropped it down onto the table in front of me, furiously pulling at the neck of his t-shirt and blowing onto his skin. "Is there a burn mark?" he asked, peering down to try and see his own chest.

I assured him there wasn't, but he went off to the downstairs cloakroom to check for himself. When he had gone I put my hand over the shiny green pendant. He was right. It was burning hot.

CHAPTER SIXTEEN

As good as it was going to get. That probably summed things up just then, between me and my father and, resigned to that fact, I decided it was best we gave each other space for the rest of the day.

After breakfast I grabbed the bunch of rusty keys from the hook in the kitchen and went out towards the summer house at the far end of the lawn. I turned the key in the lock and let myself inside, once more smelling the suspended aroma of oil paints and turpentine, the sweet earthiness of the warm wood as the building heated up in the August sunshine.

I walked over to the easels and pulled the sheet back off the first one again, revealing the smiling brown face of the artist's subject. As I looked at it, I became aware of the dust sheet clasped between my fingers and I shuddered, unable to recall putting the cover back over the canvas last time. Clearly I must have done, mustn't I? Or perhaps Phil had. Maybe he came in here and made himself a coffee after a morning spent cutting back brambles. Maybe he was the artist, slowly filling in these forgotten paintings. I had that feeling again – the feeling of being watched – and I spun around.

Something, or someone, ducked quickly down behind one of the armchairs in the far corner, out of sight. My heart thudded in my chest, my voice momentarily trapped inside my throat. I swallowed down hard. A second or two later the top of a head appeared and then a pair of brown eyes. Eventually a girl slowly got to her feet staring at me the whole time as if I were a ghost. I took a deep breath in.

"Who the hell are you?" I cried. "And what are you doing in here?"

She disappeared back behind the armchair, cowering, clearly startled by the sound of my voice, but then a moment or two later a pair of slender brown fingers gripped the back of the chair and she peeped inquisitively over at me. My eyes swept around the neat summer house, looking for some kind of weapon, should I need one. Gingerly she rose to her feet taking a step backwards so that she was jammed up against the wall.

"You...you are the same as me," she whispered, shaking her head very slightly.

I snorted. "Yeah, right. I *live* here." I wasn't some burglar or runaway or whatever the hell she was. I narrowed my eyes at her, trying to decide.

"You live here?" she echoed, her voice still no more than the softest of whispers.

"Yeah." I took a step forward, her fear making me brave, and she shot down behind the chair again. I stayed where I was, waiting for her to reappear. Eventually I called out to her. "Look, I'm not going to hurt you, okay?"

I waited. The moment stretched out, chewy and elastic. I wondered what I should do. Then the top of her head popped up behind the armchair again, followed by those soft brown eyes, her dark perfect face. She looked absolutely terrified.

"What are you doing in here?" I asked, more gently this time.

Her eyes were as wide as dinner plates. She reminded me of a Slow Loris I had seen once on YouTube eating a rice ball. She glanced nervously towards the door – the door which I realised had been locked before I came in. Then she turned back to me.

"I am waiting. And hiding," she said.

So she was a runaway. Mystery one, solved. "Hiding from who?" I demanded.

"From...him." She nodded towards the door again and I looked but there was no one there.

"Who?"

She shook her head, then her face kind of crumpled as if she was about to burst into tears. I hate seeing girls cry. I hate seeing *anyone* cry. I sighed.

"Look, it's okay. I'm not going to tell on you, all right?"

She sniffed, nodding to show that she understood.

"Are you hungry?" I asked her. "Have you had anything to eat today? How long have you been in here?" I frowned at her. "And how did you get in?"

Maybe she had climbed through a back window, I thought. I wondered where she had come from. Lower Huffingham was more than six miles away and surely if you were going to run away, you wouldn't come here of all places. She certainly wasn't dressed like she was running away.

She shook her head. "I am sorry." But I wasn't sure what she was sorry about. "Please don't tell him."

Her voice was so quiet it was hard to catch, like smoke. And there was an accent to it that I couldn't exactly place.

"Tell who?"

"The owner of the house," she said presently.

"John?"

"Yes, John," she nodded. She paused then looked at me, quizzically. "But how do you know him?"

"John? He works for my dad, kind of. He's on a retainer, you know, for when he needs him." She was looking really puzzled then so I continued. "He's my dad's lawyer."

"The owner of this house?"

"Yes. John Parker." I watched her frowning to herself, one hand up on her forehead massaging away a headache or something. Maybe she had a brain tumour too. "Look, it's okay, whatever your deal is," I promised when she seemed as though she was going to burst into tears again. "I'm not going to say anything to him, all right?"

She gave a slight nod of her head. "Thank you. He is so angry with me. I don't know what he will do."

I opened my mouth to ask her what she meant but something stopped me, the thought that maybe John Parker had a dark side; that somehow he had terrified this young woman to the point that she was hiding out in his summer house. Dark and disturbing scenarios filled my head, things I didn't want to know about. I thought I'd pretty much seen everything thanks to my dad but maybe not.

"So do you need anything?" I asked after a while and she stared at me for a moment as if the question were too huge to comprehend. "Food, or blankets or a phone or anything?" She was still just staring at me. "I mean I could get you something from over there." I jerked my head towards the window and the house beyond. "No one would know. There's only my dad and me there anyway."

She frowned then.

"John doesn't live there," I said, pre-empting the question in her frightened eyes.

"No?"

"No. He brought us down in his car but that's all. Me and my dad have got the place to ourselves for the rest of the summer."

"I don't understand," she whispered.

"Don't worry about it. It's complicated. It was my mum's idea." And I stopped talking then, thinking about my mum.

"You have a strange way of speaking," she told me.

I laughed. "So do you. I'm Adie, by the way."

She nodded. Eventually she said: "Nanteza, but they call me Nancy now."

"Nice to meet you Nancy-Now," I smiled, trying to be funny, but when she didn't get the joke I just shrugged, looking around the neat little summer house, feeling stupid and wondering what I should say now. She looked like she could easily be spooked and, if she was a runaway, the last thing I wanted was for her to take off again.

"So…" I scratched at the back of my neck. "Have you, you know, got a boyfriend or anything?" As soon as the words were out of my mouth I cringed, wishing I could have asked her just about anything else.

"Boy? Friend?"

"Yeah, you know…" My cheeks were burning now, "…someone…special?" And I felt my shoulders twitch stupidly. I've never been very good at talking to girls. Except Cara.

"Yes," she said after a while. It was a very definite yes. I guessed she was telling me not to get any ideas. "Geoffrey. His name is Geoffrey."

"Great," I shrugged. Silence. "Won't he be worried about you?"

"Yes," she said again, as definite as her last 'yes', as if these things were just occurring to her. There was something very odd about Nancy-Now.

"Don't you want to maybe tell him where you are, tell him that you're safe?"

"I can't find him." Her voice cracked then and I wondered what had happened between them. He was hardly going to be here in John Parker's summer house, that much I knew.

"Maybe I could help," I offered a moment or so later and she looked up hopefully.

"Maybe," she nodded. "Yes, please."

"Adie!" My dad's voice boomed out across the lawn just then and both me and Nancy looked at each other.

"My dad," I explained.

"Adie, you want tea? Kettle's on!"

"He's trying to find out where I am," I explained.

"Your father," said Nancy-Now. "Yes, yes, I heard him before."

I snorted. "Yeah, he can be kind of loud."

"Adie! I'm making a shopping list for Doddery-Dodds."

I shot her an apologetic smile. "I better go in case he comes over here looking for me. But I can come back. If you want anything, I mean."

She nodded but didn't give me any clue as to what she might need. I edged over to the door, looking at her as she stood motionless behind the armchair in the corner of the room.

"I'll be back." I sounded like an old Arnold Schwarzenegger movie and I grinned stupidly but she didn't smile. Strike number two. She obviously didn't have a father who made her sit and watch the entire Arnie box set one weekend. "Okay, I'll just..." I nodded towards the door and she nodded back to me but didn't speak. "Do you want me to lock it again?"

She looked at me. Or she looked straight through me. I backed out of the summer house and fumbled with the keys again, locking her in. It felt wrong, as if she were my prisoner now, my secret, but there must have been another way in and out or she wouldn't be there, I reasoned. At least this way I stopped my father barging in on her. I turned and walked back across the lawn to where he was standing at the conservatory door.

"Oh, there you are," he beamed when he caught sight of me. "Kettle's on. Come and tell me what you want to put on our shopping list for Dragon-lady next week."

I looked back to the summer house at the edge of the lawn wondering if I should tell him about Nancy-Now. He would probably be quite good with a troubled teenage runaway. At least I couldn't see him turning her over to the police.

We sat in the kitchen, Dad with a sheet of paper and a pen and a long list of things for Mrs Dodds to order from Tesco for us.

"Biscuits. You fancy biscuits?"

"Sure." I gave a quick shrug.

Dad looked up. "Your mum wouldn't approve though, would she?"

"She's not that bad." I picked up the mug of tea he had made for me. "She just doesn't let me have crisps and stuff. Not all the time anyway."

Dad wrote 'crisps and stuff' on the list and grinned at me. I noticed he was wearing the necklace again, zipping it absently back and forth along the loop of black leather, which he does when he's thinking or nervous.

"You put it back on," I said nodding to the green pendant.

"Yeah. I felt naked without it." He had two fistfuls of rings and an earring that today looked like a feather. He was a long way from naked. He took longer to get ready in the morning than my mother. He stopped playing with the pendant, straining to look down at it. "You know, I was given this on the video shoot for Desert Princess." Dad always has a story behind everything: nothing just *is*. "Some weird dude, some extra, all dressed up like a…like a witch doctor or something. You remember the video, right?"

I nodded, had seen all of Dad's videos, and listened to all of his albums over and over. Desert Princess was their last big single, shot on a beach in Dorset but made to look like the Sahara. You could tell from Dad's eyes that he was right back there now.

"Comes straight up to me, he does, and says this will help you with the voices or something like that. I think he meant the singing but that's what he said. Funny. I always remember that."

"Kind of ironic that Desert Princess was your last big hit then, huh?" I pointed out.

"Yeah, maybe."

"Maybe he bewitched it somehow. You ever think of that?"

"He was just an extra, Adie. It wasn't like he was a real shaman, or whatever the hell they're called, those African spiritual people. He was just some weirdo bussed in from Brixton, like all the others."

"So why d'you keep wearing it?"

Dad shrugged his shoulders, hooked a stray strand of hair behind the feather earring. "Superstition. I don't know. I always liked it. And Desert Princess was a good song. I think the best song I ever wrote." He paused, lost in remembering. "I wrote it about your mum. Did I ever tell you that?"

I shook my head. I feel uncomfortable when he gets sentimental and tells me how much he still loves her and all that kind of mushy stuff. They had already separated by the time Desert Princess hit the number one slot. Maybe he does still love her, I don't know. I just know that I've grown out of thinking they might ever get back together.

"You know, I'm writing again," said Dad after a while. "It's good, if I say so myself. I'll let you have a listen to it in a bit. It's the first really good thing I've written in ages. I'm going to go down that whole African road again, like I wanted before. This time see where it takes me."

"Is it another song about Mum then?" I asked and Dad smiled.

"Yes and no. I think they're all about her in some way or other."

I slurped my tea, hoped he wasn't going to get any more emotional. The last time I saw my dad cry he was off his face on whisky and painkillers and I ended up calling an ambulance. I decided to change the subject.

"Hey, Dad, what d'you know about John Parker?"

"What d'you mean? He's been my Go-To-Legal-Eagle for years now, for all of us. Never mind Ghostbusters, when you're in the doo-doo you'd better call John Parker," he grinned.

"Yeah but apart from him being a lawyer and all that, what do you really know about him?"

"I know that if it weren't for him, I wouldn't be here right now," said Dad solemnly. "And that's the truth."

Obviously if I was going to uncover any skeletons in the Parker closet, I was going to have to find them by myself. So that's what I did.

That afternoon, I lay on my bed and Googled John Parker on my iPad. It didn't tell me much that I didn't already know. Eton and Oxford educated; a bunch of degrees and letters after his name now, nothing that you wouldn't expect from a top London-based lawyer. I sighed, wondering what to do next. Then I remembered something Phil the gardener had said so I typed the name John Wetherby into the Google search bar and hit 'enter'. I waited for it to load.

The first entry was a LinkedIn page for John Wetherby, a Toronto accountant. Next came several property listings in west London for flats in John Wetherby Court. I moved the page up slowly. John Joseph Wetherby, father of Geoffrey Gordon Wetherby and Elizabeth Ann Wetherby, husband of Charlotte May Wetherby... That sounded more hopeful. I hunched over the little screen, smudged with my fingerprints in the dusty sunlight, then double-tapped.

John Joseph Wetherby was a business man living at the turn of the last century it informed me: a free-thinking liberal who worked briefly as an administrator for the Imperial British East Africa Company; outspoken against the issue of slavery, but shrewd enough to take full advantage of the cheap labour to exploit the growing global market for rubber and ivory.

I scanned down a little lower. Google was now outlining the history of the Imperial British East Africa Company which, amongst other things had been tasked with the building of a much needed railway connecting the east coast region of Mombasa to Lake Victoria. The Uganda Railway. I stopped then. That was the same railway which had brought Babu's descendants from India to Uganda in the first place. I scrolled down further, amused by the odd connections between time and place and people I had never known but who I was still linked to in some small way.

I got to the bottom of the article, unsure of what I was hoping to find. In the early nineteen-hundreds it reported that John Joseph Wetherby returned to England from the shores of Africa a very wealthy man, retiring to his newly acquired family home at Bridges End Norfolk. The name Bridges End stood out as if it had been written in eight foot tall neon letters. That was here. Bridges End Manor: John Parker's house with the ugly gargoyles and dimly lit corridors. So this was the right John Wetherby, whose deranged ghost was said to stalk the grounds after dark, unhinged by the tragic events that had occurred here. Though the article made no mention of hauntings, it did go on to detail the tragedy of the fire, confirming that it swept through the upstairs rooms of the house in October 1908, claiming the life of John's son Geoffrey. I shuddered – someone walking over my grave, as Dad always says – a synapse in my brain misfiring.

After that, concluded the article, John Wetherby became a virtual recluse, dying alone on

September 2nd 1929 in this very house. I tried to ignore the thought that was now forming like a cancerous mass in my mind. *John. Geoffrey*. Names that Nancy-Now had mentioned. I pressed the back button on the web page, returning to Google. But what if she hadn't been talking about John Parker at all? I got a sick cold feeling spreading out from my belly and down my arms. I tried to think of something else I could Google, something totally random. Slow Loris eating a rice ball on YouTube: that would do it. This was just my imagination running out of control again, spooking me the way Dad had spooked me on our first night here. I told myself to get a grip, loaded YouTube.

    Maybe she hadn't even said Geoffrey. Something else, then. I tried to remember what it could be. A name that sounded like Geoffrey. Or it could have been a different Geoffrey. Lots of people were called Geoffrey. (I ran through all the Geoffreys I knew and came up with zero). Two minutes of the cutest bug-eyed creature eating rice passed and still I couldn't shift her from my head. *Get a grip Adie*, I commanded myself. *Get a grip.* Perhaps if I went across the garden now she wouldn't be there. Wouldn't ever have been there.

    I put my iPad down and drew my knees into my chest. My brain tumour was back, wasn't it? Best case scenario: my imagination was in meltdown (the way it used to be as a kid after watching Dr Who). Worst case scenario: I was either going insane or about to die of brain cancer. Fine. At least I knew what I was dealing with. Or was there a third scenario that I was simply refusing to acknowledge? I squeezed my head between my hands, as if I could cram all the craziness back inside. Let's face it. My dad had almost destroyed himself with every chemical known to man by the time I was conceived. What poisons or broken DNA chains had been passed on to me in the process? Dad went to a shrink when he was my age too. So what with the drink and the drugs, and the inherited madness, I never really stood a chance, did I?

My heart was thumping in my chest by this point. I wasn't even sure why, just amazed at how quickly I could work myself up into a state of complete panic. But then I heard my father bellowing from the music room, swearing and shouting; shouting *my* name. I jumped off the bed and ran downstairs, through to John's office in the East Wing. What I saw there stopped me dead in my tracks.

All of my father's music equipment, his keyboard and amps and guitar had been smashed up against the far wall as if hurled in some uncontrollable fit of rage. His laptop was on the floor, along with all his papers. And my dad was just standing in the middle of the mess with his hands in his hair, scanning around him, a look of utter shock pasted onto his pale face. When he saw me he just stared.

"Adie, why? Why would you do this?"

I inhaled sharply. "What? No! Dad, I didn't."

"After everything I said this morning…" He didn't seem to hear me.

I looked around the room. "Dad…" I was going to say again that I hadn't been in here but then a sickening thought struck me. What if I had? What if I had done all of this and then just blocked it out of my crazy mind? I was bonkers enough after all.

"I know you're mad at me, mate," continued Dad, "but to do *this*?"

I could feel my whole body starting to shake. Not knowing what else to do I turned and fled up to my room.

CHAPTER SEVENTEEN

More than anything, I just wanted to call my mum and go home. How ridiculous is that, to still want to run to your mother every time things get messed up? Maybe Dad would call her now anyway. He clearly wouldn't want me hanging around anymore, not after smashing up his music equipment, and who could blame him? Had I really done that? Was I capable of such cruelty towards him? He was right, though. I *was* angry with him. I had been angry with him for years: for never caring enough to get himself straightened out; for only ever allowing me to be a walk-on extra in the crazy movie that was his life – we shared a surname and that was it; for always making me come second. But to have done all that and then to blot it out so completely? My head was starting to unravel and there was nothing I could do to stop it.

I stayed up in my room all afternoon, blasting my ears with Naughty Boy's La La La over and over again. I wished I could do that: block everything out by simply sticking my fingers in my ears and singing la la la over and over at the top of my lungs, like little kids do when they don't want to hear you. I looked out of the window at one point as the sky started to cloud over and I could just see the edge of the garden from up here and the summer house nestled amongst the far trees. I didn't dare go back there.

Eventually Dad poked his head round the door. I saw his lips moving before I heard any words and tugged the earbuds out of my ears.

"I knocked but..." He nodded at my music, "you didn't hear me obviously. I've made dinner."

"You have?" I didn't mean to sound so surprised, it just came out that way. I scrutinized his face, waiting for him to say that he had also called Mum and I was going home tomorrow. No, not going home – *sent* home.

"It's not as fancy as your stuff but it'll fill a hole," Dad told me, referring to whatever he had cobbled together in the name of dinner. "Come on." And with that he was gone again.

In the dining room, our usual places at opposite ends of the long table had been laid out, but something about it suddenly seemed ridiculous. I sat down in my seat looking at the plate of fish fingers, chips and baked beans he had prepared. There were ten fish fingers piled on my plate. He must have used up the whole packet. At the other end of the table he picked up his knife and fork, watching me closely before shovelling a chip into his mouth.

"It's from the freezer," he said and I wondered where he thought these kinds of food items normally came from.

I ate a fish finger. My father sent a squeezy bottle of ketchup skating down the highly polished surface towards me. I caught it without needing to look up and squirted a big dollop of red stuff onto the side of my plate.

"Nothing's broken," he said after a while. "Well, not anything that can't be repaired. Becky's coming over tomorrow with my old Strat. The guitar doesn't sound right somehow but apart from that…" And his voice trailed off.

I shook my head. "I didn't smash your guitar up, Dad. I wouldn't."

He stabbed a couple of chips onto his fork like he was harpooning fish. "Well mate, if you didn't, who did?"

It was a good question.

"I rang our food order through to Doddsy," Dad continued conversationally. "She said I should have done it days ago. Now we'll have to wait another week for her to bring it up."

"Guess we'll just have to make do with what's here then," I commented back.

After that, we ate in silence and then Dad went through to watch TV. I washed up the plates, looking out at the garden, wondering about Nancy over there in the summer house, wondering if I should take her a sandwich or something. I mean, that's what you would do if you were *really* harbouring a runaway, wouldn't you?

I decided to go for a bath instead, anything so that I didn't have to sit with my dad and see the hurt and disappointment in his eyes. I opened the taps fully and let the water noisily fill the big enamel tub. I fetched a paperback from a drawer in my bedroom determined to spend the rest of the evening holed up by myself and headed back into the bathroom, which was now fogged with clouds of steam. I stripped off and got in, then ran even more from the hot tap until the steam and the scorching water had deadened my brain and sent me into a stupor. I bent open my paperback and started to read, suddenly missing Cara like crazy. I never realised before how much of an anchor Cara and my mum and Nana Sara all were, holding me fast in the whirlpool of craziness that was anything connected to Dad.

I'm not sure how long I was in the water. One minute I seemed to be reading and the next I was sitting bolt upright having forgotten where I was. The water was still warm though, the paperback clasped in my left hand as before, one corner now slightly soggy. Being a quick reader, I was already a quarter of the way through. I tossed it over the side of the bath onto the floor and looked around me. In the steam across the surface of the mirrored cabinet on the far wall someone had written a single word: *leave*.

I gasped, eyes darting frantically back and forth. There was no one in here but me. I turned back to the mirror where the letters were just starting to bleed out and lose their form. I grabbed for the towel on the floor and pulled it shyly around myself, splashing water everywhere as I stumbled out of the tub. Was this Dad's idea of payback? Had he crept in here whilst I was dozing and written that on the steamy mirror? He was no stranger to practical jokes, I knew that, but this didn't seem like his style somehow. Besides, if he wanted me to leave all he had to do was ring my mother.

CHAPTER EIGHTEEN

Becky turned up on our doorstep just after eleven the next day, wielding my father's old Fender Stratocaster guitar. She was pushing her sunglasses up into her cherry-red hair as I opened the door and she looked like she'd just stepped out of a shampoo commercial.

"We have to stop meeting like this," she smiled, coming into the hallway. "How are you, darling?" She peered earnestly at me and I had to look round to see who she was talking to. Then she laughed. "You seem a bit out of sorts," she noted, and I wondered just how much Dad had told her about needing a replacement guitar.

My father appeared from the next room and took it from her, holding it by the neck like a prize fish being dangled for photographs in Anglers' Weekly. "Cheers for this Beck." He placed it carefully against the antique, don't-sit-on-that chair. Becky eyed him as closely as she had me.

"In fact, you both look like you need some cheering up," she announced breezily, glossy pink lips sliding easily over shiny white teeth. "So how about I take the pair of you out for lunch, my treat?"

Half an hour later she had pulled her little sports car into the car park of The Green Man pub in Lower Huffingham.

"A pub?" Dad seemed surprised.

"Sure. Why not? You're not exactly spoiled for choice round here." She got out of the car and then tipped her seat forward so I could unfold myself from the back. I stretched. "You're tall, Adie," she said looking me up and down and I got that funny feeling again, the one I always get around her.

There was just one other car parked in the gravel forecourt outside the pub: a battered and muddy Ford Focus. Her car sat gleaming beside it. Town versus Country. Style versus functionality. Money versus a lot less money. We went through the dark entrance of the small thatched pub and it took a while for my eyes to adjust to the dim interior. Orange lights flashed on a slot machine near the door and I could smell beer in the air. Music was playing very softly from speakers high up but it was too quiet for me to tell you what it was, I just know that it wasn't a Voodoo Mary track.

The furniture was all polished dark wood, matching the low ceiling beams, and Dad had to duck his head as we came through into the main bar area. A man was wiping glasses behind the counter. One solitary drinker sat at the far end of the bar, watching our every move, a hand cupped around his half-empty pint glass. Monday lunchtimes in Lower Huffingham.

"Is this okay?" Dad asked.

"Relax," Becky laughed, turning to me. "Grab a table." She motioned to one by the window with four chairs tucked neatly underneath it. "I'll bring you a lemonade over, shall I?" And I squirmed at how young that made me sound. "Are you serving food yet?" I watched her smile at the barman and I also watched him watching her as she passed a menu back to me at the table. She shared a menu with my father, up at the bar, both of them pressed shoulder to shoulder as they read through the food options. I suddenly wondered where Becky's official duties ended and her unofficial ones took over.

"So, this is nice." She slipped into the seat opposite and I looked out of the small leaded window, back to the forecourt and the little road beyond. No cars were passing. Dad sat beside me with a pint of zero-alcohol lager. He had asked for a lemonade, the same as me, but Becky had giggled and told him to at least have something that looked the part. So he had returned to the table with what he called 'an abomination to drinking' instead. "Anyway, now for my news," she beamed, looking at my father. "I have been in talks with a guy called Matt Peterson who, in case you don't already know, is a Canadian film-maker who is doing a ten part documentary on the history of heavy metal. And guess what? He wants to include Voodoo Mary in his footage. You know the kind of thing: get your opinion on music at the time, other bands, splice concert footage with the interview and the like."

"Yeah?" Dad grimaced as he supped at his pint. "Cool."

"I should say so!" she exclaimed, nudging him fondly under the table with her stiletto. "Let's see if we can't kick start things a bit, shall we? Get your name out there again before people really do think you've just crawled under a rock to die."

"Sure, nice one Becks," nodded Dad appreciatively.

I pulled my phone out to text Cara. Becky pulled hers out and took a couple of pictures of us across the table, leaning back in her chair to get the right shot.

"Let me see." Dad reached over and took the phone from her, studying the pictures carefully. He showed me. She'd stupidly managed to get the tops of the two pint glasses in front of my father. *I* could have taken a better picture. "I look like an alky," Dad moaned as he passed it back to her.

Our burgers arrived and we tucked into the food, conversation temporarily suspended as we all got on with eating (or at least me and Dad did: Becky ate like one of those bad TV actors – lots of chewing of not much food). Then Becky pushed her plate a little way away from her, a half-nibbled burger and most of the chips still sat there, and she started scrolling through her phone again.

"Stu says hi, by the way." She didn't look up from her screen.

I went up to the bar and ordered myself another drink. The barman angled the pump into a clean glass and a jet of lemonade sprayed out. All the time he was pouring, he was watching Becky and my dad over by the window. I started to pull some change out of my jeans to pay for it but he shook his head, turned, and when he faced me again he was holding a credit card between his fingers.

"Lady left this behind the bar," he told me with a nod towards their table. I put the change back in my pocket. "Bit flash if you ask me."

I smiled then and reached for my glass.

"Famous, isn't he?" He nodded again towards their table. "Singer, or actor or something of that nature."

"Singer." I looked at my dad sat there opposite Becky, both of them talking earnestly.

"And you?" He turned his attention back to me. "What's your connection with the likes of them?"

I faltered slightly, briefly toying with the idea of re-inventing myself: I could be a roadie, his publicist, a biographer, Becky's toy-boy boyfriend. I could be anything I wanted. "He's my dad."

"Oh right." The raised eyebrows told me he hadn't been expecting that. "Right."

He turned away and rang up my lemonade on the till, ready to add to Becky's card. Then he leaned over the counter towards me.

"So you must be the ones staying out at Bridges End Manor, that correct?" And he jerked his head in the direction of the Gents' toilet.

"Yeah, that's us."

He nodded thoughtfully. "I heard someone famous was staying there. So that's him, then is it?"

"Are you the landlord here?" I asked and he tore his gaze away from my father's table and back to me.

"Aye, that I am."

"Someone told me you were the person to talk to about the history of where we're staying."

"Is that a fact?" His eyebrows disappeared off under his hairline again. "And who was that then, telling you that?"

"A guy called Phil," I said.

"Potato-Phil?"

"I don't know. The gardener up there, at Bridges End. He told me."

"Yeah, that'll be him." He looked over at my father again as Becky suddenly burst out laughing at something Dad had just said. I think she was flirting with him. She reached across the table to touch his arm.

"How come you call him Potato-Phil?" I asked the barman.

The landlord looked at me as if I were stupid. "Why, he grows potatoes of course. Best 'tatoes this side of Norwich."

I swallowed down the razor-sharp quip I was about to make just then. Potato-Phil was probably his half-cousin or something like that and he'd only take offence.

"So anyway, he said you would know about the house?" I prompted again hoping he might be able to fill in the gaps from what I'd learned yesterday courtesy of Google.

"Interesting place, Bridges End Manor," he told me. "You know it's haunted, don't you?"

"Yeah, I heard that."

"Quite a number of people have said they've clearly seen the ghost of a man, at night, you know, walking up and down the corridors."

"That would be John Wetherby, right?"

The landlord looked at me, surprised perhaps that I knew the name. He nodded, frowning slightly.

"The very same. Died in that house, he did. Well they all did, of course. His boy was killed in the terrible blaze they had out there."

"Yeah, Phil, I mean Potato-Phil, told me that," I said.

"Oh he did, did he? Did he also tell you that some people say they've seen the house burning only to look again and find that it's not? Did he tell you that?"

"What?" I felt the blood draining out of my face and my armpits growing clammy. I made a grab for a nearby barstool and plonked myself down on it.

"Ha, you won't be able to sleep tonight now, will you?" laughed the barman. "Some believe John

Wetherby started the blaze himself, something up there he obviously didn't want people to find out if you ask me."

"Must have been serious if he was prepared to set fire to his own house," I mumbled.

"I daresay." He turned away briefly to fill another pint glass for the man still sitting at the far end of the bar then came back to me. "You're really interested then?"

I nodded, more interested now than ever. He turned round again and threw a bag of dry-roasted nuts across to me. "Put 'em on the lady's tab shall we?"

I grinned and ripped open the foil.

"Mind you, the fire, how so ever it started, was just the beginning of a whole catalogue of disasters for the Wetherby family. After the son's death the wife took ill, though everyone says she most likely died of a broken heart, that's what done for her in the end. Then the daughter was found at the bottom of the main staircase. Apparently she'd fallen but you tell me whether you think that would kill a person, a fall like that. I mean you live there, how high is it anyway?"

"I don't know." I tried to picture standing at the top of the stairs and looking down into the hallway below. I was instantly reminded of one of Dad's stories: Voodoo Mary coming out of an upstairs bar in a swanky New York hotel when Stu had drunkenly jumped over the railings at its entrance thinking it was on the ground floor only to plummet thirty feet into a foyer full of people. He actually got up and walked away but the next time they stayed there my dad said a glass wall had been put up to enclose the staircase.

"You'd be surprised what the human body can withstand."

"Would I now?" asked the barman looking amused. "Well anyway, before long John Wetherby was all alone up there in that big old house. Maybe that's just how he wanted it after all those dreadful happenings, who can say? He certainly couldn't keep staff after that, if you look at the local records, not for all his money. Housekeepers came and went but nobody ever stayed there for very long."

"He murdered his own son to stop him from leaving," declared the man at the far end of the bar. "That's what some people think."

I turned to look at him as he picked up his near-empty pint glass. The landlord just scowled.

"There was some talk about the son, yes – improper relations if you know what I mean." He nodded knowingly then glanced over to my father's table and I found myself doing the same. Becky was reaching out to trace a fingernail over Dad's tattoos as she talked. It looked oddly intimate for a PA. "Rumour had it that the son was about to take his leave of the family estate, which certainly can't have pleased the father, I'll grant you, but there's no solid evidence that John Wetherby actually murdered anyone."

"He covered his tracks then, didn't he?" said the drinker darkly at the far end of the bar. "You can't deny something's keeping his spirit from resting."

"Have *you* ever seen him?" I asked the man.

The man stared coldly back at me. "Yup," he declared, though I wasn't sure if I actually believed him.

I turned to the barman. "The son was Geoffrey, wasn't he?"

He nodded, looked back to my father's table.

"And who was the lady he was having 'improper relations' with?" I asked.

He shrugged, frowning at me as though he thought I were mocking him with his talk of 'improper relations'. Then he picked up a towel and started to wipe the length of the counter forcing the drinker at the far end to pick up his pint glass as he did so.

"No record of her," he concluded finally.

"And what does that tell you?" The drinker replaced his glass on the bar top.

"That it happened a long time ago?" I suggested.

"That she wasn't the same as them. She belonged below stairs, if you get my meaning, a serving girl. Scandalous at the time, of course!"

"As if that kind of thing wasn't going on in every great house up and down the country." The landlord turned to grin at me. "They just kept it behind closed doors more than they do today. Nowadays you put everything all over the internet like it's something to be proud of." He flicked the towel up over his shoulder and looked again at my dad and Becky over by the window.

I stayed at the bar until they were ready to leave. The landlord pressed a button on the till and it spat out a long white bill and she nodded as he put her credit card into a little hand-held device and offered it over to her. I watched her punch in the code with those long perfectly manicured fingernails and then she handed it back to the landlord complete with glossy smile and perfect flick of shampoo-ad hair.

Next thing we were crammed inside her little sports car and heading back to Bridges End Manor, back to a house where people saw fires that weren't actually there and ghosts roamed up and down the corridors after dark. My palms grew sweaty the closer to the old house we got. If I wasn't losing my mind, then I was living in a house with the undead. It hardly seemed much of a comfort.

CHAPTER NINETEEN

Becky spun the car round in the forecourt in front of the ugly gargoyles and left the engine running as Dad got out, pulling his seat forward so I could get out too. Then he bent down to look in at Becky.

"Not coming in for a cuppa?"

"No. This place gives me the creeps. I'm going to head straight back to London. Call me if you need anything, as always. Ciao darlings!"

"See ya Beck." He thumped his palm down twice on the roof of the car and with that she sped off, back to civilisation.

We walked up to the front door, Dad rummaging in his jeans pocket for the house keys but as we got to the entrance, we noticed the door was already slightly ajar and my father looked at me accusingly.

"Did you not close the front door properly, Ade?" He pushed on it and went gingerly into the hallway. This was the same hallway where the daughter had died. I imagined her lying on the brown and yellow tiles at the foot of the stairs in front of me. "Hello?" Dad's voice broke through my ghostly imaginings as he looked about him.

"I think there's something not right with this house," I said softly, following his gaze as he looked about us, east to west, west to east.

"What? Why d'you say that?"

As he spoke the heavy oak door creaked shut behind us and I looked at him. "Because of that," I hissed.

Dad laughed. "That was just the draught, Adie. At least there's nobody out here to rob us or murder us in our beds."

"How can you be sure?" I had already dropped my voice to a whisper. "How do you know it's not some crazy stalker fan who's tracked you down all the way out here? They could be waiting for you now, upstairs!"

But my brain told me that some crazy stalker fan was going to be the least of my problems.

Dad opened his mouth to tell me I was imagining things but then stopped, maybe seeing the worried look on my face, and he smiled. "Come on then, let's go arm ourselves with something and give this house a sweep through, eh?"

As he handed me a spatula from the kitchen I knew he wasn't taking this as seriously as I'd hoped. He took a carving knife from the drawer for himself.

"And what am I supposed to do with this?" I waved the spatula at him. "Give them five minutes and then flip them over?"

"You're a kid. You don't get to play with knives." He threw the carving knife from one hand to the other, then back again and I could see this all going horribly wrong, as with so many things connected to my father.

Next thing I knew, we were creeping through the house, room by room, my dad crouched like a soldier, making hand signals to me that I knew he'd only seen on American war films, but he was suddenly playing Rambo and I was trailing miserably behind carrying a stupid plastic spatula in one hand, wondering why everything had to be such a big joke to him.

"Clear!" He sprung up from his crouching position by the door and ran into the next room, pressing his back against the wall like they do in cop films, scoping out the bad guys.

I followed him through into the giant library watching as he dropped to his knees again at the far door to the music room, motioning silently for me to do the same. I reluctantly crouched down. He slotted the knife handle between his teeth then scrambled on his belly to the door.

"Clear!" In an instant he was through, back on his feet and slicing wildly at the air with his knife like he was hacking his way through dense jungle.

I sighed and was about to walk through to join him when the great eight-foot door literally swung shut in my face. I grabbed at the door handle but it was locked tight.

"Dad?" I shouted through the wood, pulling frantically on the handle.

I could have sworn the whole room seemed to take a breath in just then, sucking the walls towards me. Moments later I felt all the hairs on the back of my neck stand to attention, an electric charge in the air. I turned around very slowly and watched in horror as a small coffee table levitated unsteadily off the floor. A patterned vase that had sat there moments before slithered off and bounced onto the carpet.

"Dad!" I turned back to the door pulling desperately on the door knob, pummelling my fists against the wood. "Dad!"

I felt the small table whiz past my right ear and crash hard into the wall behind me. I covered my face with my arms, ducking to the floor in case any more missiles came my way. One of the legs had broken off the table and I scrambled further away from it as though it were possessed, tucking myself into the far corner of the room, eyes closed tightly and my head buried in the crook of my arm.

"Jesus, Adie!" My father stood in front of me with a broken table leg in one of his big, ringed hands. "It was just a bit of fun. What d'you go and do that for?" He picked up the rest of the table. "What if this is one of those antique jobbies of John's?" He shoved the leg towards the table as if he could cram the two mismatched pieces together but there was no way they could be fixed: the wood had sheared off in jagged splinters.

I stayed where I was, crouched on the floor, trembling, peeping anxiously over my arms at him, still with my stupid spatula clasped in one hand.

"Oh really, Adie, what am I gonna say to John now?" sighed Dad.

"I didn't..." I started and then heard how lame that sounded.

Dad thought so too. "Yeah, whatever." He threw the table and broken leg back down before noticing the vase lying on its side a little way away. He stooped to pick it up but as he did so it shattered in his hands. "Shit!" He dropped the sharp pieces back onto the carpet, sucking on his palm, then looked at me, still cowering in the corner. "For God's sake, just clean this lot up, will you?" And with that he stomped upstairs presumably to go and bandage his freshly cut hand.

"Dad!" I didn't want him to go; didn't want him to leave me alone in this creepy room with its flying tables; didn't want him to venture alone upstairs just in case there actually *was* a psycho stalker still lying in wait for him in his wardrobe. But, as always, he did exactly what he wanted to do and left me there, sitting uselessly in the corner.

I waited, commanding my muscles to relax again, forcing my legs straight out in front of me. I spread my fingers over the patterned carpet. Time seemed to slow down.

"Leave..." At first it sounded like the wind through the tree branches but I was indoors and there was no wind. I sat there straining to hear through the heavy still air. *"Leave...Leave..."* I looked up. The sound had become a voice. A man's voice. *"Leave. Leave! Leave!"* As my breathing got louder so did the command, growling and angry. I moved my neck stiffly, not wanting to but expecting to see some ghostly apparition standing there. The room was empty. *"Leave!"* My legs felt hollow and I knew they would never be able to support my weight even if by some miracle I *could* make myself stand up again. *"Leave this place!"* The voice now rang in my ears. I imagined I could feel the ghostly breath that accompanied them, rancid and rotting against my face, and I clamped my hands down firmly over my ears, burying my head in my knees and scrunching myself tightly into a ball.

"No! No! No!" My own shouting drowned out the ghostly voice. "No! I can't hear you, la, la, la. La, la, la."

"Adie?"

I lashed out blindly, kicking at my father who stumbled backwards a couple of steps.

"What the hell is wrong with you?" he demanded.

I sat there in my corner, looking wildly around me. There was just me and my dad in here. I listened for a moment: nothing but the grandfather clock ticking in the hallway and the frightened rasps of my own breath. I looked up at my father. He put his hand out and yanked me roughly to my feet.

"You want to explain what's going on here?" he asked.

"Your hand's bleeding," I said dumbly.

He frowned hard at his palm, at the thin red line of blood, and sucked on it again. "It's nothing, I always bleed like this. Now what on earth has got into you?" He narrowed his eyes at me like he couldn't fathom me out. "Come on. Let me go and run this under a cold tap first."

I followed as he walked down to the kitchen, shaking his head slightly and mumbling to himself. "Look Adie, I know I haven't always been here for you, haven't always paid you the attention I should, but you don't have to..."

"Dad!" I cut him off. "That isn't about me wanting attention, all right? If I want your attention, I'll paint myself purple and dance naked down Oxford Street, okay?"

"What's that supposed to mean?" He ran his hand under the kitchen tap, blood and water dancing over the white enamel. It was an unusually deep cut considering how it happened. I looked back out of the window. You couldn't see the summer house from here but I was acutely aware of it nevertheless. I watched the tops of the tall oaks rippling in the afternoon breeze, anything so I didn't have to see the red streams gurgling down the sink hole. "Well go on then," ordered Dad briskly, winding a tea towel round his hand like a tourniquet. "I'm right here. Talk to me! You've got my undivided attention."

"Can't you feel it?" I turned to my father. "It's like the house doesn't want us here."

"Oh for God's sake Adie," my dad exclaimed, "you keep talking like this and I'm gonna get you to see a shrink."

Suddenly the swamp of anger was back and churning over in my stomach.

"What, like you did, you mean?"

Dad instantly stopped patting his hands dry and glowered at me. "What?"

I looked away. It was something we had never spoken about before.

"You don't know what you're talking about." He threw the tea-towel down on the kitchen table. "Forget this. I'm going for a walk." And with that he stomped out the back door.

I watched him tramping angrily across the lawn and wondered where he was going. As he disappeared off into the distance I realised that we were still no closer to discovering whether there really was a psycho stalker hiding out upstairs. And if there was, Dad had pretty much left me alone to deal with it. Same old, same old.

CHAPTER TWENTY

When he was out of sight, I helped myself to a kitchen knife and went to investigate upstairs. The main staircase creaked under my weight and I stood for a moment at the top, glancing nervously around me. It was the middle of the afternoon in August. The sunshine filtered in through the landing window, dust particles floating in the air like dirty water. It shouldn't have been scary but my heart was tearing through my t-shirt. I looked over the bannisters. Would a fall from this height kill a person? In an instant I had jerked around, knife held out in front of me. Was it my imagination again or had a cold hand just pressed between my shoulder blades inviting me to find out?

Beads of sweat broke out on my forehead. I wondered if I should wait for Dad, though something told me he wasn't coming back any time soon. When he gets in a strop like that he can be gone for days, time suspended inside an alcoholic vacuum. Thankfully, unless he was prepared to walk six miles back to the Green Man, that couldn't happen here. I listened to the house. A sudden gust of wind rattled the window behind me and I turned again, then again, not sure of which side to protect first with my trembling kitchen knife.

Edging slowly along the corridor, I paused outside each room to listen: for ghosts or burglars, I still wasn't sure. Then I'd turn the door knob, which invariably slipped against my sweaty palm, and finally burst noisily into the room, hoping to scare away anything that might be in there, kitchen knife stabbing wildly at nothing. I checked in wardrobes and under beds as I knew that these were the places fans tended to hide – the undead I was less sure about – room after room – and with each one my heart thumped that bit heavier, that bit faster. My head was swimming with panic by the time I came to my own bedroom, ghoulish spirits dancing before my eyes, every creak of the wooden floorboards a deathly voice. *He's not a bad man. Not a bad man. A bad man. Bad man.*

I pushed back the door – nothing – edged inside – a movement to my left – I jumped back and my reflection in the wardrobe mirror did the same. I sank weakly onto the bed as my legs finally buckled beneath me. This was ridiculous. If I had seen either a ghost or a burglar by this time I'm pretty sure I would have pissed my pants.

That night I ate dinner by myself, leaving Dad's helping plated up and next to the microwave for when he came back, assuming, of course, that he hadn't actually gone out to catch dinner with his own bare, caveman hands. Then I washed up by myself and watched TV by myself and finally went upstairs to bed by myself. He was clearly hacked off at me big-time for knowing about his visiting a shrink and I felt guilty for ever bringing it up.

I kept all the lights on thinking that this would be the best way to hold any malingering spectres at bay. Phil had reported people feeling trapped in this house yet I was experiencing the opposite: a ghostly presence that was most definitely intent on our departure. Did this make it any less real, I wondered? Perhaps it was simply a hallucination conjured up by my broken brain. Unable to sleep I texted Cara and then spent half an hour trying to send it. Next I read nine chapters of Charles Dickens' *Hard Times* (they're particularly short chapters) and, still not sleepy, finally pulled out my iPad and checked in online.

Cara was in Spain for a week with her folks, no doubt eating fish and chips and ice-cream, sitting in English style cafes with Union Jacks flapping merrily outside. I already knew more about Spanish food than she ever would. Paul wasn't on social media for some bizarre reason but if I knew him, he'd probably be spending the summer in his bedroom. I clicked on favourites – Voodoo Mary – and brought up the band's profile. Dad's face was at the top of the page and I was surprised to find Becky had posted that picture of him from earlier this afternoon, the one with the pint glasses in it (though I noticed she had cropped me out completely). Her post read simply: Craig parties on! I thought that was odd but had bigger things occupying my mind just then and finally flipped over the cover on my tablet, shutting it down, and wriggled under the duvet, eyes still wide open on the look-out for phantom invaders from the netherworld.

I stayed like that for the longest time, staring hard at the wall opposite, willing it to remain where it was, my eyes then flitting, frightened, to the wardrobe thinking that I'd seen something, but being greeted by the empty reflection of my bed in the oval mirror on the door; and all the time listening, listening to the wind sneaking in through the gaps in the old sash window, listening to the creaking of each individual mattress spring, the water pipes gurgling, listening hardest of all for the sound of my father coming back in, safe, not mad at me anymore. Karma, Nana Sara would call it, worrying about him like she and Mum worried about me that Sunday night a couple of months back when I ended up in a stolen car with Curtis Laycock.

At some point my eyelids started to burn and I could no longer keep them from closing as I drifted off into a thin, troubled sleep in which the shadows of angry ghosts passed menacingly beyond my door. Some hours later it was the brightness which dragged me back to consciousness and for a moment I couldn't remember why I was sleeping with all the lights on, like I did when I was really small and the monsters had seemed equally real.

"Adie, please wake up. I cannot stay long."

I blinked to find Babu standing at the foot of my bed. With the light shining through him he had an odd, translucent quality, an image only partially loaded.

"Babu! You're here. You're real?"

"Adie, you are in great danger," he whispered urgently.

"I am?"

The main light in the room flickered a couple of times.

"Yes, you and your father." He paused as the light blinked on and off and on again. "The spirits in this place are in dreadful turmoil and I fear that you are both right in the middle of it all. You must take care."

"Do not judge him too harshly..."

This was a new voice, a female voice, and I looked around to see who it might belong to but could find no one else with us.

"Babu..." I started but at that moment heavy footsteps sounded in the hall, slowing and then stopping directly on the other side of my door. I paused, holding my breath. The bulb in the centre of the ceiling gave a loud pop, plunging the room into darkness and I gasped. The door was now clearly illuminated by the light from the corridor glowing all around it. I saw a shadow lingering in the gap at the bottom.

"Dad?" My voice was just a whisper. I heard it shake, betraying my fear, and turned back to Babu but he had already vanished into the darkness. "Dad?" The word caught in my throat as I looked again to my closed bedroom door.

The shadow, whatever it was, faltered then moved slowly away, further along the corridor. I lay stiffly back down in bed, head strained on the pillow watching the strip of light and wondering how I could arm myself against things that probably weren't even real.

The following morning I stumbled bleary-eyed down to the kitchen to find my father already up, though he was wearing the same clothes as yesterday so I had to assume he hadn't yet been to bed.

"I'll put some washing on today," I mumbled, nodding at my father in his yesterday-clothes.

"Yeah, good. Good idea," he replied, frowning distractedly.

It would never have occurred to him that washing clothes was something else he had to do for himself. Edith, his housekeeper in North London, takes care of all that kind of stuff for him. People always take care of things for him. Maybe this summer it was *my* job and I was just one more entry on his payroll.

"So where did you get to yesterday?" I held the kettle under the spluttering tap, hoping that the question sounded like a general enquiry rather than an accusation. You could hear the water pipes rattling and banging deep inside the walls.

"Just went for a walk," Dad replied, watching me switch on the hob and throw a couple of tea-bags into clean mugs from the cupboard.

I figured he couldn't stay mad at me if I made him a fresh cup of tea.

"Adie…"

"Dad…"

We both spoke at the same time and then both stopped and looked at each other and half-laughed, awkward and self-conscious. I wondered if this was what Paul was like with his old man, or Cara with hers. Or Beethoven with his.

"No, let me go first," said Dad and he took a big breath as if this was something he needed to steel himself for. "I'm sorry for storming out like that. You just took me by surprise, is all. I didn't think you knew about me visiting a shrink."

I shrugged. "I'm fairly sure I wasn't supposed to know about it if I'm honest. It was just something Grandpa let slip one time when Mum and me were up there."

Dad seemed somewhat taken aback. "My father told you?"

"Well I don't think he meant to," I was quick to assure him. "He misunderstood something Mum said." When I looked up Dad was staring at me, puzzled, so I rushed on with my explanation. "She made a comment about me being mad, you know, angry-mad and I guess he thought she meant cuckoo-mad and he just let that slip about them taking you to a psychiatrist when you were my age. I'm pretty sure he never meant to tell us."

"I wasn't cuckoo-mad," Dad mumbled, hurt, a moment later, and I found myself apologising all over again. "And what were you so mad at that she mentioned it to him?"

"Oh you know..." And I shrugged again, didn't want to admit that it was my own father I was mad at most of the time.

Dad knew anyway and dropped his eyes. "Sorry. Sorry. I keep saying that, don't I?" And I shrugged again. The kettle started to steam and I leaped up to make tea, glad to break the heavy, awkward silence that had now muscled in between us. "I'd forgotten about that time, actually," Dad said, watching me as I moved round the kitchen. "Yeah, I was the age you are now or thereabouts," he sighed. "For a while I thought I was going crazy."

I leaned into the spaceship fridge. "Join the club."

He was zipping his pendant quickly up and down his neck as I turned round, about to ask him if he'd put milk on our next shopping list, but he wouldn't meet my eyes now. "I was hearing voices, you know?" he continued softly, "Seeing stuff that wasn't really there."

Instantly I had frozen to the spot, the carton of milk dangling from one hand. Dad was eventually forced to look up.

"Well close the door, Ade, you're letting all the cold out."

I fumbled the fridge door shut behind me and slopped milk into the waiting mugs. I placed one down in front of him, sat opposite, paused. He was staring into his tea now. "So...er...I mean what...what kinds of things were you seeing?" I asked eventually.

Dad shrugged his broad shoulders through the black concert t-shirt. "I'm not sure exactly. Sometimes horrible things, like accidents and stuff."

The image of a man trapped underneath an open-topped bus flashed back into my mind. I blinked it away.

"My mother blamed it on the music I was into," he smiled wistfully, "you know, heavy metal? I had this Judas Priest album as a kid and if you played one of the songs backwards, it was supposed to summon the devil or something."

"And did it?"

"I never wanted to ruin the record to find out," he said, honestly.

"So what happened?" I hardly dared ask but the words were out of my mouth before I could stop them.

Dad shrugged. "I kind of got into music in a big way after that, and of course all the other things that went with it." He flashed me a guilty smile and I knew he was referring to his drug habit. "And the voices just faded away. The doctor put it down to teenage hormones and an overactive imagination."

I sat opposite him at the kitchen table, cold all the way through to my bones. My pulse started to race as I felt my mouth cranking open in slow motion, almost against my will. Was I actually, finally, going to tell someone? "But...but I get the same thing," I admitted in a small, strangled voice. He lifted his head sharply and we both looked suspiciously at each other.

"What are you saying?" he demanded.

I dropped my eyes shyly, nervously. "Lately, well, I've been seeing things too, like people that have been run over, people that I think might have died…" And I glanced up at him, still staring back at me, his mouth gaping open in disbelief.

I was Craig Cooper's son after all. Those were my eyes staring back at me. "I see things that no one else can," I said quietly. "And I hear voices too. I've even talked to Babu a couple of times." I inhaled sharply. I had forgotten how to breathe properly.

"Babu? Yeah? And what does he say?"

"He says we're in danger here, in this house."

Dad frowned back into his tea. "Oh, he does, does he?" But for once he wasn't making a joke about it.

"I thought I was going mad but now I don't know what to think."

I counted my heart beats – one, two, three, four, five – before my father spoke again.

"Yes you do," he replied. "You think you're seeing ghosts, same as me."

I opened my mouth to say something else but no words came out.

"That's what you think," said Dad. "You just don't want to admit it. I spent ages not admitting it to myself. That's probably why I ended up on a psychiatrist's couch. After that I blotted *everything* out, even what I had for breakfast yesterday." He stared at me. "But I lost your mum, and you in the process. Hell, I nearly lost everything, not just the voices."

"I didn't smash your guitar up," I said after a while and Dad just nodded.

We drank our tea in the kitchen. In the silence all the other sounds seemed a hundred times louder: the gurgling plumbing, and the whirring of the fridge. Then one of the old bells on the wall gave a short dull ring and both me and Dad looked at each other, wide-eyed. My belly swelled with icy fear.

"That could just be the front door," I said eventually but neither of us moved.

"It could be Becky," whispered Dad.

Still neither of us moved. Silence.

"Have you seen what she's posted online?" I asked him and he nodded. "Why would she do that?"

Dad opened his mouth to offer some sort of explanation when the little bronze bell tinkled again. We both looked at it.

"I'll go check." Dad got slowly to his feet.

I jumped to mine. "I'm coming with you."

In the hallway Dad paused momentarily before tugging open the heavy front door. At first there seemed to be no one there. Then, seconds later a man picked his way out of the flower bed to our left having been peering through the library windows.

"Who are you?" Dad demanded suspiciously as he stood there in front of us, dusting himself down.

"Hello there. I'm Mickey Laing."

"You can be Mickey Mouse for all I care," snapped Dad. "What are you doing snooping through our windows?"

"I'm a freelance reporter." He pulled out a small white business card from his trouser pocket. Dad batted it away from his outstretched hand and it fluttered to the ground like a dead butterfly. "I was hoping to do a piece on the hell-raiser Craig Cooper. That'd be you."

"I'll raise hell on you if you don't get out of here," my father warned, "I'm on holiday with my son and I don't want to be disturbed." Then he turned to me. "Adie, go get my gun."

I nodded and stepped back from the door, the reporter instantly doing the same, hands up in a gesture of surrender.

"I'm giving you five seconds to get back in that heap of junk over there, then I start shooting out your tyres."

Mickey Laing only needed four.

Dad shut the front door and grinned at me, still pressed up against the hallway wall out of sight. Then the smile faded. "How d'you think he found us all the way out here?"

I shrugged.

"And why now?"

I shrugged again. "Something to do with Becky's post?"

"Yeah, maybe. Think I need to have a word with her about that."

We paused, listened. The grandfather clock ticked steadily, measuring out time.

"Do you think we should pack up, get out of Dodge?" My father narrowed his eyes at me.

"You mean leave? I don't know. It's definitely like someone or something doesn't want us here. Do you not feel it too?" I asked him.

Dad gnawed on his bottom lip, sighed. "I guess I feel something." His hand went to his throat, to the little green gem stone he always wore. "I thought it was the effects of laying off the booze and what have you. You know, that can make you a bit skittish too. And when it's really bad you can even see things." He stopped abruptly. "But it's different here. I know that. I've been hearing a girl's voice, singing to me some times."

"Nancy-Now!" I gasped. "I need to go and talk to her."

My father frowned. "I know my brain is fried but I'm lost. Who the hell is Nancy?"

"I think, I thought, I mean..." I shook my head, trying to force some order into my brain. "Well at first I thought she was a runaway. Now I think she might be the reason the house doesn't want us here."

CHAPTER TWENTY-ONE

As we walked through to the kitchen I explained about my meeting with Nancy-Now. We both looked out over the lawn towards the summer house.

"I'll go with you," offered Dad.

I shook my head. "No. Let me just speak to her alone first. She's kind of flighty."

My father reached for the shiny green pendant around his neck. "It's getting warm again." He held it away from his skin. "I know it sounds crazy but I think it could be her, trying to get my attention."

I realised nothing sounded crazy to me anymore.

"Maybe it wasn't ever supposed to help with your singing," I said, remembering the story he had told me about the guy who gave it to him on that Dorset beach. "It was to help with the other voices, exactly as he said."

Dad looked at me but didn't say anything.

"I won't be long." I slipped out of the back door, feeling my father's eyes watching my every move.

"I've got your back, Ade," he called.

I could now see the summer house nestled in the trees at the bottom of the garden and I tossed the big rusty bunch of keys almost happily in my hand, something only now dawning on me: I was no longer doing this – whatever this was – alone. And if Nancy really was a ghost, then she was definitely more Casper than Candyman. Friendly ghosts I could deal with. Maybe, in time, I would even come to relish this thing that my father and I both shared.

The tops of the trees rustled with the morning's breeze. I could feel the warm sun on my face, the breeze rippling at the bottom of my t-shirt. It was certainly beautiful round here, I told myself cheerfully, as though only just noticing it for the first time. But as I walked towards the bottom of the garden the breeze grew steadily stronger – pushing against me now, more a wind than a breeze – forcing me back. Clouds scudded fast across the sky as if a storm was suddenly closing in but it was all happening way too rapidly, as if time had been fast-forwarded. I bent into the wind, eyes watering, and I narrowed them as cold tears rolled down my face, blurring my vision.

I was halfway across the lawn when I faltered, wondering if I shouldn't just go back to the kitchen and wait for this mini-tornado or whatever it was to pass. But by now I could neither go forward nor back. As soon as I lifted one foot I knew I was going to be blown away, such was the strength of the gale whipping all around me. Something was wrong. This was no ordinary storm. At that moment, the keys were torn from my hand and I watched in amazement as they spiralled up in front of my face almost as if they were feathers caught in a draught.

"Nancy!" The wind took the voice from my mouth.

I turned round to look back at the house and reassure myself that my father was still there when something fast and black suddenly bolted through the sky straight for me. In the next instant I felt my feet being ripped off the dewy grass and then I too was flying through the air like a piece of litter.

"Dad!"

I landed back down with a jolt. There was no sound. One moment I could hear the roaring of the wind in my ears and the next moment there was nothing. In its place a soft mist swirled around me, like an early morning fog, slowly clearing to reveal a wooden footbridge arched over what I assumed was a stream, though the misty cloud prevented me from seeing for sure. I opened my mouth in a yawn, trying to pop my ears like I do when I've just been at a concert and my head is jammed with cotton wool.

The cloud, which was tinged with pink and yellow as if the morning sun was streaking through it, continued to swirl around me, obscuring the rest of the garden and the house and the trees. I wasn't even sure if I was in the same garden anymore. Maybe the wind had picked me up and dropped me in a neighbouring field somewhere. There was just this sloping wooden bridge stretching off into the hazy distance and absolute silence. I put my hand on the bridge to make sure it was not just a figment of my imagination. The rough wood felt reassuringly solid beneath my palm. I took a step forward, then another. But after that I stopped and looked back, searching for the house or other familiar landmarks. The cloud drifted up around my legs so that nothing was visible. My thoughts were muddled and my head hurt. When I put my hand up to my temple, I drew it back red with blood. I stared at this with a dislocated but rising sense of panic.

Beyond the curve of the bridge came a movement and a man now appeared, walking slowly towards me. I became aware of the stillness all around us, the lack of sound; no hot, no cold; no breeze; nothing. He seemed surprised to see me. I opened my mouth to ask him where I was but for a moment was too scared to speak, in case I really had gone deaf. He now stood just a couple of metres from me. He was dressed in a tight-fitting, waist-coated suit, the shirt collar fastened high up around his neck. It looked uncomfortable. He had a moustache and hair that was slick with gel. I somehow knew that he wasn't from my time.

"What just happened?" The words were thick and muffled in my ears but at least I could hear them. "And who are you?"

"My name is Geoffrey, Geoffrey Wetherby. And you?" His voice was soft but formal, no trace of an accent.

"Adie Cooper." I only just managed to stop myself from calling him 'sir'.

"What are you doing here?" he asked.

"I don't know." I looked around me, the thin wisps of cloud spiralling softly like candy floss. "One minute I was going to see Nancy and the next..."

"Nancy?" He faltered at the mention of her name.

"Nancy. Nanteza?" I remembered that was what she said her name was, but they called her Nancy now, and I had tried to make a stupid joke of it.

"Nancy! Where is she?" Geoffrey took a step towards me but his eyes were looking past me, over my shoulder, into the cloud.

I nervously stepped back.

"She's in the summer house," I told him, instinctively looking at my hand for the bunch of keys I had been holding just a minute ago, but they were gone.

"I have been waiting for her," said Geoffrey urgently. *"Though she never came. He told me she had left, gone for a ship to take her back to her country but I knew in my heart that she would never leave without me. Yet, all this time and still she doesn't come for me."*

"I don't understand. Who? Who told you?"

Geoffrey's grey eyes settled on mine. There was a sadness deep inside them. *"My father. John Wetherby."*

"John Wetherby?" I looked up again. "That could be the man Nancy said she was hiding from. In the summer house. She said he was very angry."

"Yes! That sounds like him. He was indeed incredibly angry."

"And she mentioned you too, by name."

"She did?"

There was a sudden hopefulness to him now and I nodded. "But I still don't understand. What happened with your father?"

"He could not accept us. Nancy was his, you see, and in his eyes I was taking her from him. We were going to travel back to Africa together, but of course he would never allow it."

"So you were planning to run away? With Nancy?"

Geoffrey nodded his head sadly. *"We had no other choice."*

"And what happened?"

Geoffrey paused, as if it were painful to remember. *"Take my hand and I will show you what I can."*

He stretched out his palm towards me, as if he was giving me a high-five. I nervously raised my own hand up, wondering if he would feel solid in the same way that the bridge did, or if my hand would simply sail straight through his. I laid my palm gingerly against his, instantly noticing the dryness of his skin. The next thing I knew we were no longer on the bridge but in Dad's room back at the house, staring out of the window. In front of my eyes a pair of white arms came up and drew the heavy curtains across my vision, then bent down and lit the waxy stub of a candle that was sitting on the bedside table, bringing the match up to my face to blow out.

Although I had a sense of Geoffrey still standing close beside me, I was somehow looking through someone else's eyes. The arms stretched out again, to the top of the wardrobe, bringing down a big leather suitcase and in that moment I glimpsed Geoffrey in a freestanding mirror against the far wall. He wore a loose white shirt, only buttoned halfway up, a pair of braces dangling at the waist of his trousers. He was throwing clothes hurriedly into the suitcase laid open on the bed, emptying the drawers of his dresser in great handfuls.

My vision now went to the door, which had burst open, an older man lurching in. He had clearly been drinking, staggering and swaying towards the other side of the four-poster bed.

"What in God's name do you think you are doing?" he bellowed.

The hands stopped packing only briefly.

"You know full well what I am doing. I am leaving tonight for Folkestone. With Nancy. There is nothing you can do or say to stop us." The voice seemed to come from somewhere within me.

"Poppycock!" exploded the man. "Over my dead body will either of you leave this house!"

"Then that can also be arranged," replied Geoffrey coldly.

"Do you forget who you are addressing?" the older man now growled.

"No father, I do not," answered Geoffrey.

"Then perhaps you forget that Nancy is rightfully mine? Or that, had it not been for me, the two of you would never have met. I didn't save her from a life of slavery simply to lose her all these years later."

"No, you merely traded one type of slavery for another," said Geoffrey.

"You speak out of turn," snarled John Wetherby menacingly. "I would strongly advise against it."

My vision was now firmly fixed on Geoffrey's father swaying slightly on the other side of the bed.

"Nancy has served you well these past years, father. She has repaid that debt many times over," came the voice somewhere deep inside my chest.

"I have treated her like a member of my own family," John Wetherby exploded indignantly, "offered her more than she could have ever dreamed that day when she stood, pitiful and cowed, on the dock in Mombasa, waiting to be bought, a mere chattel, a child barely weaned from her mother's milk. She should be grateful I saved her from that life of hardship and pain."

"Yes, I am sure she is grateful but the fact remains it is *I* whom she now loves and nothing is going to change that."

John Wetherby laughed cruelly, staggering slightly. "Love? Don't talk to me about love. They cannot feel love in the same way that you or I can. Don't be a fool, boy. This fancy will pass."

"It is not a fancy. I love Nancy and I know that she feels the same. And if we cannot be together here then we will return to her home and make a new life for ourselves there. I do not seek your blessing father, or your permission, for I know that neither will be forthcoming, but hear this: you will not stop us."

"The hell I won't!" roared John Wetherby rounding the bed and appearing to lurch towards me. "Besides, she's already gone."

"Gone? Gone where?" Geoffrey snapped.

"Gone home. Homesick. Bought herself a passage back to Africa. That's how much she loves you, boy."

"You lie!" roared Geoffrey.

I saw the man strike Geoffrey hard across the face, once, then twice. Thankfully, although I could feel the jolt of the strike, I couldn't feel the pain that must have accompanied it or smell his stale whisky breath, his face inches from my own. Geoffrey appeared to be just standing there, and I saw his hand creep up to one cheek, head lowered. I noticed the shoes he was wearing, the pattern on the carpet. The next thing I was aware of, looking out through Geoffrey's eyes, was the wall and the ceiling as he was now stumbling backwards, then a thud as I assume his head must have hit the side of the dresser. As he slithered to the floor I saw his father's hand, still clenched tightly in a furious fist.

"I told you! You will not leave. Your place is here," John Wetherby shouted at the slumped down figure of his son.

I could feel the confusion of thoughts going through Geoffrey's mind as he struggled to get up from the carpet. He looked at his father who now turned back to the bed and heaved the half packed suitcase against the wall as if to emphasise he was indeed going nowhere. I saw it crash against the bedside table knocking over the candle there. Geoffrey's eyes, and therefore my own, were now watching his father stumble at the door, fumbling with the key, the door slamming, and the key grinding in the lock on the other side.

"I told you," shouted the voice from the other side, thick with alcohol, "You go nowhere without my permission!"

Then the eyes travelled back to the corner of the bedroom. By now the flames from the candle were licking hungrily at the edge of the heavy curtains. I felt Geoffrey stumble as he tried to stand, saw his shoes on the carpet again, a hand outstretched unsuccessfully to stop himself from falling one more time.

"Oh no!" I said the words out loud, in my own voice, automatically reaching my hand out to where I sensed Ghost-Geoffrey standing beside me and in an instant the vision had gone and we were back on the bridge.

"I'm so sorry," I whispered. "What can I do?"

He peered at me through the swirling mist. *"Find Nancy for me. Tell her that I am here, waiting for her."*

"But that was…" I stopped. Did he even realise that what we had just witnessed happened more than a century ago? "I don't think your father wants me talking to her somehow." I glanced around me, trying to locate the summer house through the thin trails of cloud.

"Well tell him it was an accident," urged Geoffrey softly. *"I know he didn't mean for it to happen in that way. Tell him…well, just tell him I forgive him. Maybe then he can finally rest."*

"But why can't you tell him?" I asked.

Geoffrey shook his head. *"When you cross this bridge you can never return."*

I looked down at my trainers on the old wooden slats, suddenly scared that maybe I too would be trapped here, unable to return.

"Adie? Adie! Wake up."

I heard my dad's voice somewhere deep inside my head. My temple throbbed painfully. I looked back at Geoffrey.

"So you're telling me that Nancy isn't…she hasn't, I mean she's still back there in…?" But I didn't know where 'back there' was.

"Perhaps she doesn't know. Perhaps she's scared. She doesn't realise that I am still here, waiting for her, just as I promised." The mist rose up between us. *"I will always wait for her."*

"Adie, please son, wake up."

"Tell her for me," said Geoffrey and with that he turned and walked away up over the bridge and out of sight. I tried to call to him but I had no voice. Clouds filled my mouth.

The next thing I could feel was myself being bumped up and down but I couldn't see why or how.

After that there was softness and blackness and finally I sunk a little deeper into the abyss between consciousness and something else.

CHAPTER TWENTY-TWO

"I've called an ambulance."

For a while it was as if he was talking a foreign language to me. Nothing made sense inside my head. I put my hand up to where the pain was worst but Dad pulled my arm away.

"It's still bleeding."

I tried to sit up but that was impossible too. My body felt as though it had been filled with concrete.

"Jesus Adie, you gave me a hell of a scare. You've been out cold for fifteen minutes."

I tried to touch my forehead again but once more Dad stopped me. I swivelled my eyes around, keeping my head where it was. I was in the lounge, lying on John Parker's floral sofa. My head pounded. I closed my eyes and saw the mist and the bridge and the man.

"Geoffrey!" I opened my eyes. "I spoke to him. He died in the fire but it was an accident."

Dad peered worriedly into my face. "Okay just calm down, son. The paramedics will be here soon enough. Don't get yourself too worked up. That was some bump on the noggin you got."

"We were on the bridge, I saw him, I spoke to him." I wanted to explain but with my pounding headache and jumbled thoughts it was too hard. "I need to see Nancy. I have a message for her."

"Just lie down and stay still." Dad pushed against my shoulder as I tried to sit up. "For God's sake

Adie, what do you want me to do? Knock you out cold again? Just relax and do as you're told for once."

I remembered John Wetherby punching his son and knocking him against the cupboard, saw once more how the suitcase clipped the side of the cabinet and toppled the candle over, the curtains catching alight, saw them burning – but this time it was the image of my dad lying on his bed asleep, a smoked-out joint between his fingers. The pictures were all muddled and confused inside my mind.

"No Adie, don't go to sleep again." Dad was shaking me now.

My brain rattled painfully inside my skull.

"Come on, talk to me," he urged, "anything, anything you like, even your garbled gobbledygook, Adie, just stay with me."

I forced open my eyes. "What happened?"

"You got hit on the head by a couple of tiles from the shed roof. That wind! It just came out of nowhere."

I tried to touch my forehead, where the pain was greatest, but instantly Dad pushed back my arm.

"I saw the tiles just whip off the roof and next thing you were down, out cold on the grass."

"The bridge, what about the bridge?"

Dad didn't seem to hear me.

"God, what's taking them so long?" He looked at his watch and I could tell he was trying not to panic.

A part of me wanted to just close my eyes and slip away from the persistent throbbing in my head but I was scared too, remembering my trainers on that footbridge, the footbridge that only went one way...

"Am I wearing my trainers?" I asked and Dad looked at me as if I was mad.

Then he laughed. "You look great son, don't worry about what you're wearing, you look great as always, same as your old man."

"No, I didn't mean..." But it would take too much effort to explain.

Dad laughed again. "You know what my mum always used to say? She told me to wear clean underpants when I left the house every morning to go to school, you know, just in case I had an accident. Like that was the most important thing: having a decent pair of shreddies on!"

"Dad..."

I tried to remember getting dressed this morning. I was wearing my Calvin Kleins. I think I remember being pleased about that.

And then the paramedics arrived.

CHAPTER TWENTY-THREE

The next thing I remember with any clarity is being in a hospital bed, somewhere noisy and very bright. Dad was with me.

"Can I go home now?" I asked him.

"Soon," he promised. "They just want to keep you in for a few hours more, for observation."

"No, Dad. No!" I sounded like a whiny little kid.

"You don't seem to realise how serious that knock on the head was," he told me. "You could have died."

"But I'm okay now."

"I'll believe that when I hear it from the doctors," he said with a heavy sigh. "You just lie there and get your strength back." Dad looked around him. "I suppose I should call your mum."

"Really?" I tried to sit up then thought better of it.

"She needs to know."

He looked away as he said it and I realised what he was thinking: that she would assume he had messed up again, left me in danger, that somehow this was all his fault. She would think it was the same old, same old. She would want me to come home.

"Don't tell her," I whispered. "Please. Not yet."

Dad looked back at me, unsure.

"Please," I begged. "Later. You can tell her later, when this is all over."

He finally nodded. "Okay, if that's what you want. I'll get you home first."

I smiled and closed my eyes.

There was a bed for me in a children's ward where I lay, dazed and confused, having been told to rest, but whenever I closed my eyes as if to sleep they came and prodded me awake. This continued all afternoon. And when dinner was dished out I realised I was expected to stay overnight. My headache was still there but fuzzy and muffled, presumably with whatever painkillers they had fed into me. At one point I opened my eyes and Babu was sitting in the plastic chair next to my bed. I smiled and closed my eyes again. Next time it was Dad sitting there. I smiled and closed my eyes again.

Kids cried all night. I would have rather been put on an adult ward, with a bunch of farting old men, than here with these crying babies and Disney characters on the walls but this was where they stuck me. The nurses had cartoons on their plastic aprons. I cringed every time I saw them. And they just laughed at me like I was the biggest baby there.

When I awoke, early the next morning, Dad was nowhere to be seen. I got served breakfast in bed with all the other children and told that as soon as the doctor had seen me I could go home. I felt for the bump on my forehead, now enclosed in a thick padded bandage. I was just finishing the last of my toast and staring out of the window at some city roof tops that were clearly miles away from Bridges End, wondering where I was, when a movement at the foot of my bed caught my eye. I turned to find Dad and Becky standing there. I was pleased to see Dad but annoyed to see Becky.

"Hey," I nodded at the pair of them, self-conscious that she should catch me in a hospital gown.

"How are you feeling?" asked Dad and I shrugged and told him I was okay.

I wanted to talk to him privately, away from Becky, but guessed he'd had to call her: her and her little sports car, her and her efficient organisation of all his affairs and mishaps. Maybe my father's account with Addison Lee wouldn't stretch as far as the wilds of Norfolk, but Obliging Becky obviously would. A kid started to scream really loudly just then so they excused themselves and said they would wait for me in the day-room at the end of the corridor, leaving me to pull on my clothes behind a thin blue curtain with Aladdin and Simba looking on.

It was two hours later that I was finally discharged, the doctor giving my father a verbal summary of observations to pass on to my family GP in case the incident got lost in the NHS computer network, Dad nodding earnestly, trying and failing to hold it all inside his head. Then there were clear instructions as to what to do if I felt nauseous or my vision started to blur again and Dad nodded a little more determinedly. Becky led us down to the car park at one side of the building, bleeping open the car doors with her key fob.

"Maybe Adie should sit in the front," said Dad as she pulled back her seat for me. "You know, in case he feels sick."

We swapped places and I strapped myself into the front seat, Dad folded in awkwardly behind. Becky slotted her phone into the holder on the windscreen tapping in our destination to the Sat-Nav app. "Back to the middle of nowhere it is," she announced and started the engine.

Music filled the car. I groaned and she instantly apologised and switched it off. I leant my head against the window and closed my eyes.

"Head still sore?" she asked and I grunted back a yes and she left it at that.

We drove through an unfamiliar city which gave me a familiar pining for all that comes with city living: people and bustle, kebab shops and clothes shops, noise, colour, cars. After a while though we had left it behind again and found ourselves out on narrow country roads with high hedges on either side, leading us back to our ghost-house.

"So we saw what you put online," I muttered a little later.

"Uh huh?" Becky was concentrating on driving.

There was a pause. "Did Dad tell you we had a reporter come to the house?"

"Really?"

I glanced round to my father but he had his eyes closed, head tilted back against the headrest.

"Yeah." I looked at Becky. Becky looked through the windscreen. "Bit of a coincidence, wouldn't you say, him just turning up like that?"

She glanced over at me, then back to the road. "Meaning?"

I didn't want to have to spell it out. I hoped my dad would jump in and say something but maybe, what with the engine noise and his rock-and-roll damaged ears, he couldn't make out what we were saying.

"There's no need to cop an attitude," she told me snottily. "It comes with the territory as I'm sure you know." She glanced over to me again. "There's no bad publicity, Adie, just *no* publicity and that's worse than anything that ever gets written about you. Just ask Justin Bieber!"

"So did you run it past Hannah and Lenny first?" Dad leaned forward in his seat. He must have been listening after all.

Hannah and Lenny were, amongst other things, the publicists for Voodoo Mary. Becky looked uncomfortable, tightening her grip on the wheel.

"Craig, do you even realise how many people are on the Voodoo Mary payroll these days, getting paid for doing jack shit? At least I'm being proactive, getting your name out there again. I care about you. I'm not ready for you to reach for your pipe and slippers just yet."

"Neither am I," grunted Dad. "But I could do without being labelled a hell-raiser all over again."

"You're just the latest in a long line of rock 'n' roll hell-raisers. You told me yourself you grew up listening to some of the greatest hell-raisers of all time: The Stones, Ozzy, The Sex Pistols and it never did their careers any harm!" There was an uncomfortable silence. "And it's not as if you're writing anything new these days so what else is there for them to report?"

Dad sank back in his seat. "I am as it goes." He ran his hands through his long blond hair, elbows scraping the roof. "Maybe you and I should have a chat when we get back."

I looked out of the window, allowing myself a slight smirk. That told her.

We had now reached the metropolis of Lower Huffingham. Dad demanded she stop so we could pick up milk and bread. Becky got out and pulled forward her seat, making it clear that if he wanted to do a grocery shop, he needed to sort it out for himself. He disappeared into the small post office shop and she slapped the seat back, plonking herself down in it but keeping the door open. I could smell the flowers from the hedgerows. It was going to be a hot day.

"You okay?" she asked me after a while.

"Do you really want to know or are you just worried what I might do to your upholstery?"

"Don't be like that," she sighed. "I do actually care about your dad and you, Adie. We've known each other a long time, haven't we?"

I shrugged and looked out of the window wondering what my life would be like with Becky as a stepmother. It was not a good daydream.

CHAPTER TWENTY-FOUR

I left Becky and my father to have their 'chat' and went upstairs for a bath and to change into some clean clothes. Afterwards, I stood and wiped my hand across the steamy cabinet mirror, examining the bandage on my forehead at close range, then brushed my teeth, starting to feel normal again. I glanced up from the basin.

Behind me, a face stared angrily back through the glass, a face I now recognised as John Wetherby's.

Dropping the toothbrush I grabbed for the edge of the enamel, too scared to turn round and look at him directly, yet too frightened to turn away. Our eyes locked in the mirror. As the moment dragged uncomfortably on, my arms started to shake, hands grasping the sides of the basin so tight that my fingers were going numb.

"It was an accident," I squeaked through a mouthful of minty foam "He...he says he forgives you." I swallowed down the toothpaste.

There was absolutely no reaction on the face. I wondered if he had heard me. This was supposed to be the moment that, absolved of all guilt, he rests in eternal peace and the sun comes out and birds twitter in the trees and all is well again. Happy Ever After. The End.

"Leave this place!" he hissed and the ghostly voice seemed to cram itself into every corner of the

bathroom, reverberating against my eardrums. *"You are not welcome here."*

I tried again, my heart now crashing inside my chest. I looked into his cold dead eyes through the mirror.

"G-Geoffrey, your son, he told me to tell you…"

But at that point a high pitched shrieking sliced the air like a burglar alarm and I was forced to clamp my hands over my ears against the noise. There followed a sharp cracking sound and the mirror, just inches from my face, splintered. John Wetherby's angry expression was suddenly multiplied and distorted in the cracked glass. I turned very, very slowly but the bathroom, thankfully, was empty again.

Back downstairs, dressed in fresh clothes, I found my father in the kitchen butchering a loaf of bread in the name of sandwiches. He looked up as I came in. I was pleased to note that Becky was nowhere to be seen.

"Hungry?"

I nodded and he pushed over one of the doorsteps of fresh white bread towards me.

"Lay your dirty clothes out and we'll finally get round to putting some washing on," he said. "I'm down to my last pair of D&Gs."

I sat at the kitchen table and munched through the cheese and ham sandwich while Dad made us both tea. He had grown almost domesticated over the last twenty-four hours.

"I saw him," I said, swallowing hard, "John Wetherby, just now, upstairs in the bathroom." I glanced at my dad, then back down at my sandwich. "I take it you didn't hear anything?"

Dad shook his head.

"He told me we weren't welcome here. Then there was this high pitched kind of scream and the mirror in the bathroom just sort of shattered. After that he disappeared."

"I guess it's time we packed our bags," mumbled Dad, zipping his gem stone pendant up and down the leather bootlace round his neck while he waited for the kettle. "I don't want us staying here if it's not safe."

"You'd call John Parker and get him to pick us up?"

"Sure, in a heartbeat. I don't want you in danger, Adie. I'll call him straight after lunch."

"You don't think I'm going mad?" It felt necessary to check.

"Of course not." He looked almost annoyed that I'd had to ask the question. "You forget, I've been there too." He stopped playing with the pendant and screwed up his eyes.

"Is it her? Is it Nancy?"

He popped the pendant back inside his t-shirt. "I think so." He turned to the hob to make the tea. "I guess it never really left me after all, this gift or curse or whatever it is. It was here all along."

"You know if we leave now, nothing will get sorted," I pointed out. "The spirits in the house won't rest. Just more people will come and go through here, and no one will want to stay. Nothing will ever change."

"That's not our problem."

I thought of Nancy hiding in the summer house for the last hundred or so years, Geoffrey waiting patiently for her on the bridge. "Isn't it?"

Dad turned back and placed a mug down in front of me.

"I've never done anything with this...this...this thing that we both apparently have," he told me. "I was too busy pretending I couldn't hear the voices. I don't know what we're supposed to do now."

"We could go and talk to her," I suggested.

But given what had happened last time I tried, that might not be as straightforward as it sounded.

"Is that what you want?"

I shrugged. "It doesn't feel right to just do nothing."

Dad sighed, less convinced.

"What's the point of having this..." I paused, searching out the right word, "...this ability if you then don't do anything with it?"

Like a singer not singing or a painter not painting. If it was inside you then it was already a part of who you were, whether you liked it or not. Sooner or later you had to embrace all the jigsaw pieces that made you into your own unique – and sometimes crazy – whole.

Once we had washed up the plates and mugs, and loaded the washing machine, we stepped out of the back door and stared at the lawn beyond.

"The keys! I lost the keys." I turned to Dad who, smiling, dangled the rusty set from one finger.

"I picked them up. They were in the grass beside you."

I remembered the way they had blown through the air in front of my eyes, someone's desperate attempt to stop me from entering that summer house. This afternoon, though, there was not a breath of wind. It was a perfect summer's day. The sun glinted through the tall branches of the trees, dancing warmly over the grass. The summer house sat at the bottom of the garden, its windows reflecting back the still summer sky. A perfect picture of an English afternoon.

"Come on if we're doing this," said Dad and stepped determinedly off the back step. He started to stride down towards the bottom of the garden.

I ran a couple of paces not wanting to be left behind. We were halfway across the lawn when the sky clouded over again and the wind started up. This time, though, there was no waiting around to see what would happen next.

"Quick! Run!" Dad barked and sprinted off across the grass.

A sliver of demonic lightning split open the sky.

I raced after him as a branch sheared away from one of the tall trees and came tumbling towards me. I threw myself up onto the decking in front of the summer house as it flew past. Dad fumbled with the set of keys, desperately trying each one in the lock, hands shaking, but this time it was nothing to do with alcohol or drugs.

"Hurry!" I shouted, not that it was necessary to tell him, but I was scared. The sky was almost black now and the wind was lashing through the trees like an invisible whip. My head throbbed with the sudden exertion.

The lock gave way and Dad almost fell through into the little wooden shed. I scrambled after him and we both pressed ourselves back against the door, shutting out the unseasonable storm. As our breathing slowed we looked around us, our eyes growing accustomed to the shapes and shadows in the dim light. The two paintings stood on easels at the far end, covered once more with their ghostly dust sheets. It occurred to me then that the girl's face in the unfinished painting, well it was Nancy, wasn't it? I had a clear vision of her sitting for Geoffrey out here as he painted her, their relationship deepening with each layer of oils on the unfinished canvas.

Dad found the light switch on the wall and flicked it on. I blinked. It flickered and fizzed. I blinked again. The wind howled around the summer house and its wooden walls creaked in protest.

"You've seen the Wizard of Oz, right?" said Dad, attempting to joke.

I ignored him and stepped a little further into the room, looking instinctively to the armchair in the corner, behind which Nancy had cowered last time I was here.

"Nancy?" My voice shook a little. "Nancy please, I need to speak to you. Nancy are you here?"

Outside the wind screamed unnaturally. Inside the summer house everything was markedly still and normal by comparison, the eerie eye of the spectral storm.

"I've spoken to Geoffrey," I announced moments later.

If the words sounded ridiculous, I could no longer hear them. I had been speaking to dead people for months now. This was just something I was going to have to live with, I realised – like cancer, or brown eyes, a stutter or being bad at maths.

The top of a woman's head now peeped over the back of the armchair, a familiar pair of large brown eyes in a pretty, brown face. She was about to stand up when she noticed my father with his shaggy blond hair, black t-shirt and checked shirt tied loosely around his waist, his chunky silver rings and tattooed forearms, silver skull earring dangling from one ear, and she disappeared back down behind the chair with a frightened whimper. I took another step forward.

"Nancy it's okay. This is my dad. Remember I told you about him?"

After a while she peeked back over at us. She appeared like a cartoon character, half a face and eight slender brown fingers gripping the back of the armchair. She eyed my father curiously. Neither of us dared move in case we scared her again. Eventually she straightened up, her head now cocked to one side.

"Your clothes are most strange. Do you come from the circus?"

Dad looked at me, then down at himself grinning broadly. "Well d'you know what? I think I actually do."

Nancy giggled slightly, then stopped abruptly and turned to me. "Geoffrey. You've seen him, spoken to him?"

I nodded, unsure of how to phrase what I needed to tell her.

"And? How is he?" she demanded.

"He says he's waiting for you. On the bridge."

"But we were to meet here." She seemed confused. Maybe she hadn't realised that she was dead. Maybe she didn't actually know what had happened to her. Maybe that was the key to her still being trapped on this earth. I wondered what *had* happened. Had she simply pined away over the years when he didn't come for her? But this wasn't an old woman standing before us. Something else must have happened to her and I thought again of John

Wetherby, furiously trying to hold his family together. I looked back to Nancy.

"I, er...the plan's changed," I told her but then another thought occurred to me: how did you find the bridge when you didn't know where to look for it? And how could I break the news to her that both she and Geoffrey had perished more than a century ago? I guessed time lost its meaning in that other realm.

"But, but I can't leave," she sobbed. "Mr John will not allow it."

My dad looked worriedly at me. I stared back at him. Neither of us had any idea what to do next. Just then my father's hand shot up to his neck, the pendant growing hot once again. He pulled it away from his skin.

"What is that? Let me see." Suddenly Nancy had emerged fully from behind the chair and stood boldly before us, made curious by the green gem pendant around my father's neck.

I could now see that Nancy was wearing a pale blue floor-length dress with a long white apron over the top of it, a servant of this house from over one-hundred years ago but just as real to me and my father now as she had ever been. She edged towards him, towering over her as he was, and reached nervously up for the pendant. Their hands brushed together and Dad gasped as though he had received an electric shock, closing his eyes momentarily and then opening them again, looking at me with a new understanding.

"Oh no," he whispered and I knew that in that split second he had seen something terrible.

Nancy didn't seem to realise as she was carefully examining the gem stone.

"This is from my country," she said. "I have one too. How did you come by it?"

"This weird dude gave it to me," said Dad and she stopped examining the pendant to look at him now, frowning, probably unable to follow his strange way of talking. "He said it would help me hear the voices more clearly or something."

"Yes." She looked quizzically at him, then at the green stone with its dark bands and swirls. "In my village we say that this stone is a pathway to other worlds, a bridge back to this world for spiritual energy. It is very powerful." She stopped speaking then as if a thought was only now dawning on her. "You heard me through this stone."

Dad nodded and Nancy instantly let the pendant slip from her fingers as she stepped away from us both, a look of horror breaking over her face.

"Nancy..." I stepped towards her but she moved back again.

"No." She shook her head slightly.

"Geoffrey, remember Geoffrey. He's waiting for you. We can help you find him."

The thought of her past love seemed to revive her a little and she nodded, swallowing down a muffled sob.

"Adie." Dad put his hand on my shoulder. "Maybe if I could speak to you outside?"

Something in his voice made me think better of refusing. I turned back to Nancy.

"We'll be back, okay? Just stay here for a little longer. Then we'll take you to Geoffrey."

I hoped that was a promise I was going to be able to keep.

Dad turned back to the door, opening it to reveal a beautifully tranquil summer's day with no sign of the storm that had been raging just minutes before. He strode out onto the decking and closed the door behind him.

"You saw something, didn't you, something about Nancy?" I said.

Dad screwed up his eyes, his hands at either side of his head. "She went into that shed over there to get something for the guy, John what's-his-name, her boss," he told me. "But she didn't come out again."

"How come?"

Dad shook his head. "I couldn't see exactly. She went in, then the door swung shut and everything went dark. All I saw after that was a man's face and the flash of something silver and then I was back in the summer house with you." He swallowed down hard. "I think he was waiting for her. I think he murdered her."

"Jesus! He killed his son's girlfriend, got rat-arsed and then managed to kill his own son too. No wonder his spirit is in turmoil."

"I don't think we should mess with him," warned Dad.

"But how can we help Nancy? How can we help her find a way out of this without confronting him first?"

"You want me to call an exorcist?" Dad's eyes were popping out of his head.

"I don't know! I haven't exactly been in this situation before."

"Me neither." Dad shook his head. "So what d'you think Becks would say if I asked her to find us an exorcist?"

I shrugged, didn't want to think about her right now. "Like she says, there's no such thing as bad publicity. I guess she'd make something out of it."

Dad was serious again, his hand at his throat, clasped around the pendant once more. He looked to the edge of the lawn.

"I'd say the reason Nancy is trapped here lies in that outbuilding over there."

He was looking at the shed with the bikes, with the cold clammy hand, with the overwhelming sense of evil and I had absolutely no desire to go back inside there.

"No, Dad…"

"Don't ask me how I know, Adie, but whatever we're looking for, I'll stake a year's royalties on it being in there."

CHAPTER TWENTY-FIVE

My father and I were now walking across the lawn towards the stretch of tumbledown outbuildings at the far edge of the grass, him walking with a sense of purpose, me with a sense of foreboding. By the time we reached the door to the first shed my breath was catching painfully in my throat and I felt as though I were suffocating inside my own body.

"Please Dad, don't," I begged.

"You stay here then," he muttered.

"No!"

I didn't want to go in. I didn't want *him* to go in. I had this weird sense of stepping outside my body and watching the pair of us, here at the edge of Bridges End Manor, somewhere in the middle of nowhere, in deepest, darkest Norfolk and I thought: how can this be happening to Craig Cooper, world famous Voodoo Mary front man? I had to be tripping because this was a whole new level of crazy. But Dad was already turning the rusty door handle and in that instant I was back in my own body, standing close enough beside him to feel the hairs on his arm prickle up against mine.

"I guess we're ignoring all the stuff you said about not putting me in danger, right?" I whispered but he didn't seem to hear me as he stepped inside.

I followed him in, smelling the same damp scent of hay, of moist rank earth. The light from the hole in the roof shone down at a crooked angle, illuminating the tools hanging on the stone walls in its dusty yellow light-shaft. The air was cold against my skin. I took a deep breath in but as soon as I did it was as though it was being sucked straight out of me again, and I had to draw back a couple more desperate lungfuls. I shivered. The temperature appeared to be dropping. In front of me my father scanned around, one hand clasped protectively around his throat and the look of searching for something on his shadowy face.

The shed door creaked slightly and we both turned, alarmed.

"Think you can find something to prop that open with?" Dad asked in a wavering voice.

"Yeah, sure."

I saw a couple of breeze blocks lying close by and pushed them up against the wood with my foot. Then I turned, noticing how the light from the open door softened the black shadows of the shed to a fuzzy browny-gray. I peered over to my father, standing to one side of the shaft of sunlight streaming down from the hole in the roof, his spotlight, the singer about to burst on stage as soon as he received his cue.

"I guess, whatever happens next, we'll find out exactly what this thing of ours does," said Dad glancing over his shoulder to me.

"Be careful."

I didn't know what else to say. The words sounded inadequate and small. Dad just nodded and looked about him: four stone walls with long rusty nails for hooks; the old gardening equipment hanging there, sleeping, waiting; empty sky stretching above us through the hole in the roof, impossibly far away, and the cold smell of something unnatural slowly filling our nostrils. Dad took a couple of uncertain paces towards the centre of the barn and then dropped to his knees. I assumed some malevolent force must have felled him and searched wildly around me for the hoard of marauding ghosts but there was just the empty darkness of the old outbuilding staring back at me.

I turned again to my father who had now placed one hand flat on the ground in front of him, spreading his long silver-ringed fingers out over the earthy floor as if listening to some deep, other-worldly vibration.

"Here!" he whispered and then began to claw frantically at the dirt floor with his hands, like a dog.

"Wait!" I grabbed a shovel off the wall and handed it to him. There seemed no point in making this more difficult than it needed to be.

He got back to his feet and started to dig. As I looked up I thought I glimpsed someone else standing there in the shadows, watching; more than one person in fact, as if suddenly there was a whole room full of people just staring as my father now cut a great hole into the ground with his shovel. I squinted into the shadows trying to find distinct outlines, shapes and faces: Babu, yes; a young woman; an older woman, they were the only ones I could make out clearly, then just indistinct shapes, all of them standing on the edges of the shadowlands. And although they were dead I could sense a powerful echo like a heartbeat, waiting anxiously now as Dad, oblivious, sank his spade deeper and deeper into the packed earth.

I sucked another frightened breath into my lungs and forced my attention back to my father, digging furiously now, the hole getting deeper and wider with every grunt and shovel load of stale earth.

After a couple more minutes, he threw the shovel aside, sinking back to his knees, and scraped with his fingers, stopping suddenly with a gasp. He brushed the earth aside to ease something out, using a kind of rocking motion to dislodge an angular object that had been buried for a very long time. He held it up in his hands for me to see and I could plainly make out that it was a skull.

"Please tell me that's not…" I started but could not finish.

The years had picked it clean of any flesh or anything other than its bare skeletal remains. I swallowed down an urge to be sick as Dad rotated it slowly in his giant hands.

"Oh God," he breathed softly and I looked to see what he had seen.

One side of the head had been caved in, a crumbling dent left where once upon a time…

"*He* did this," whispered my father. "He did this to her."

I stumbled backwards as the sick urge re-surfaced.

"No, this isn't…It can't be…" But I couldn't get her name out.

"Nancy's skull, yes," Dad whispered back. "John Wetherby coshed her over the head with something and then buried her out here."

"No!" I couldn't connect the small damaged skull my father now held in his hands with the woman, whole and solid and perfect, that we had been speaking to ten minutes earlier in the summer house.

My father has skulls in his house in north London, I thought, made of stone or glass, which he uses as candle holders. Surely this was just another of those freaky ornaments? Then I remembered Nancy and lost my battle with the urge to hurl. I spun on my heel, puking up against the far wall. Dad placed the skull gently down on the earth beside him and dug a bit further into the newly excavated hole, pulling out another clean bone, then another.

"Oh Christ. Poor bloody kid." He laid them all out to the side of him in a small, pathetic pile.

I guess if I had ever really thought about it, I might have assumed there would be an intact skeleton for us to unearth, the way cartoon cats strip flesh from fish and pull one long skeleton out of their mouths. But Dad was uncovering odd dislocated bones: a shoulder blade here and an arm bone there and a bit of spine...

"I think..." Dad wiped a grubby hand over his face, which was contorted in pain, "I think afterwards the man chopped her body up and buried it, trying to cover up his crime." As he spoke, he reached into the shallow grave and pulled out another long slender bone.

I was glad it was dark so he couldn't see my face.

Dad burrowed a little deeper into Nancy's long forgotten grave and pulled out something else. I leaned in to see. His fingers uncurled and sitting in his palm was a small dark stone on a broken, rusty chain. "Her necklace," he breathed and instinctively touched the one round his throat.

So it really was her. We both paused to look at it nestled there in his huge muddy palm, just a dark spot in the centre of his hand. Then Dad put the pendant into his jeans pocket and turned back to the final forgotten resting place of Nancy-Now.

I crouched beside him, unable to help, sickened by the idea of reaching inside with my own bare hands and pulling out another fragment of someone I felt that I actually knew. It would be like reaching into the belly of a person and hoiking out their liver. How was that even possible unless you were a surgeon in a bright shiny operating theatre, saving a life not excavating it? But Dad had found another fragment of bone, possibly a rib and he laid it gently on top of the small heap of other bones, Nancy's earthly remains. I felt the cold against my face and briefly thought I was going to pass out. There was a creaking noise and I looked towards the door, terrified that it was about to swing shut and trap us here for all eternity with Nancy's skeleton. The sunlight streamed through and I could see the solid loop of chain on the wall swinging gently over the rough stone as if caught in a breeze, except no earthly breeze could shift anything that heavy. I looked back to my father as he wiped his hands around the hole in the middle of the floor checking for any more bone fragments.

A sudden scraping of metal on stone – I looked up to see the loop of chain unfurl itself from the nail in the wall which held it, a metal snake coming to life. It now came whipping through the air towards us. There wasn't time to shout a warning to my father. I lurched forward, pushing him out of the path of the chain and he fell with a grunt to one side as it zipped between the pair of us, missing me by centimetres, and then slithering to a halt across the far side of the floor where it smacked up against the wall. A garden rake which had been propped there fell to the ground with a bounce. We both paused. Dad went to get up when there came another almighty crash and all the other garden tools, including the massive chainsaw, fell down from their hooks in unison and clattered to the floor.

"What's happening?" I cried, still crouched beside my father.

"Let's get out of here!"

But at that moment something else came whipping through the air just feet off the ground and we both dived out of its way, a long handled scythe twisting like a propeller through the dark, embedding itself in a crevice in the stone wall opposite. I got shakily to my feet but stumbled backwards as my heel sank into the edge of the hole Dad had just dug, the soil giving way so that I fell backwards into the shallow grave. I scrabbled to stand up but at that moment there was a noise like thunder, or an underground train, and it seemed to shake the whole of the outhouse. Dad turned, his arm outstretched ready to pull me back onto my feet but suddenly the gap between us had grown and I realised, to my absolute horror, that I was sinking – the ground crumbling beneath me, around me, a crack a foot or so wide splitting the earth in two. I could feel my foothold dissolving under my weight as I scrabbled desperately against the sides of Nancy's burial plot trying to get a purchase somewhere. But I was definitely sliding further down now, the ground shifting beneath me as a giant sinkhole yawned open.

Noises roared in my ears, the earth itself breaking apart, sucking me in, as I flailed around in my search for something to hang onto...

"Adie!" Dad's hand grabbed onto my wrist, gripping so tightly it was like an iron bracelet. My free arm now thrashed around trying to find something else to hold on to but every time my fingers reached out and felt for a knot of earth it crumbled away, dry and useless. Beneath my feet I could no longer feel solid ground, just cold air around my ankles as I dangled into the dark space that had broken open beneath me. I tried to swing one leg to the side of the pit, searching for a foothold but there was nothing solid that could take my weight and I knew that neither of us could hang on much longer.

Dad's face was close to mine, him lying flat at the edge of the crater and me dangling into what was now a deep, dank hole, the pair of us connected by one hand but slowly succumbing to the inevitable pull of gravity. Noises. The panting of my breath. Dad screaming at me to hold on. Just hold on! Someone laughing. Madly. Me whimpering now, knowing that I couldn't, couldn't hold on, my arm was being wrenched out of its socket. Dirt falling all around me, in my eyes, my hair, my mouth. The pain and the terror and the need to hang on but all the time the terrifying realisation that neither of us could keep this up for more than a couple of seconds, Dad's hand now starting to slip out of mine...

"You will not take him!"

"Dad!" ...So many things you want to say at that final moment as the last grain of sand passes through the hour glass...

And then, all of a sudden, another hand, cold, yet solid, had gripped hold of me, fingers curling round my other wrist, and then another and another: one hand now tucked under my armpit, another pair around my waist, two more pushing up against my legs, keeping me from going under, somehow defying the inexorable pull of the earth, and then Dad was hauling me back out of the sinkhole and he kind of flung himself and me backwards onto the ground scattering Nancy's bones, the skull rolling crookedly into the darkness like a misshapen football. I jumped away from them as if they were scorching hot. Dad caught hold of me as I lashed out, trying to get to my feet, but my legs were no longer able to support me and he hugged me into his chest as the pair of us scrambled further away from the edge of the pit, gasping and spluttering.

"It's okay, I've got you."

The cold hands fell away one by one, just leaving Dad's grubby palm pressed firmly into the back of my head, each of us holding onto the other because neither of us had the strength to stand up alone just then. When I finally peeked out from my father's t-shirt all I saw through the heavy brown shadows was Babu, standing there a little way away from us, smiling, nodding slowly as if to say 'you're all right'.

"Thanks," I squeaked.

"Come on, let's get out of here." Dad half-pushed me towards the door and I stumbled back into the light, taking greedy gulps of fresh air as I emerged into the sunshine and flung myself face down onto the grass.

I lay there for a couple of seconds, filling my lungs with summer air, feeling the blades of grass beneath my fingers. I moved my head, about to say something to Dad, when I realised I was alone out here: my father wasn't beside me. I turned around, looking desperately back into the dim shadowy outbuilding. I could just see his outline inside. He was gathering up Nancy's bones in his shirt.

"Dad, come on!" I scrabbled onto my feet then stood helplessly in the doorway as he disappeared further into the dark shadows by the wall, feeling for the skull somewhere lost on the floor. "Please Dad!" But I just couldn't make myself go back in there. "Please! Come on! It's not safe!"

He reappeared seconds later, a shirt full of bones, and a dented human skull cradled carefully in his arms: Craig Cooper. Voodoo Mary front man. Hell-raiser. Ghost-whisperer. My dad.

CHAPTER TWENTY-SIX

"Are you okay?"

We were both still sitting on the lawn, me with my head on my knees, Dad with a scatter of bones beside him. I felt my father's hand on my shoulder, felt the familiar tremble through his arm, this time matched by my own. We both just sat there, trying to gather our thoughts.

"What *was* that?" I asked eventually.

"A sinkhole? An opening into the pits of hell? The end of the world? I don't know." My father looked at the pile of pale bones scattered in the grass to one side of him, nestled in his old checked shirt.

"And what are we going to do with…with…" I nodded at the bones.

Dad frowned, reaching automatically up to his throat. "We'll find a way to get Nancy home, don't you worry."

I sighed, every last drop of energy leaving with that same breath. If, at that moment, the sinkhole had cracked open the lawn, I would have had to let it swallow me up too. I stared at my father. He seemed shattered as well, face streaked with dirt and sweat.

"You know if the press get wind of this you'll be known forever as Craig Cooper the grave-robber," I pointed out.

"Becks'll be happy then," Dad shrugged. "A new angle for her to exploit."

A flock of crows was coming in to land on their favourite tree top branches. Dad watched about twenty of them all fighting for the right perch.

"You know they call that a murder of crows?" he commented absently.

I was too tired to think of an answer. A murder of crows. Only my dad would know that. Chips of golden sunlight flickered and flashed through the branches, leaving splashes of warmth on my face.

Sitting there, I was struck again by the awfulness of what had happened to Nancy-Now, a young African girl, supposedly rescued from a life of slavery to come and work at this grand house in Bridges End, Norfolk, thousands of miles from home. Told to be grateful that she now belonged to John Wetherby, hailed a so-called liberal, who had spoken out against slavery, yet who had still taken that life away, a life he had bought and then thrown away again all those years later, just because he couldn't bear for anyone else to lay claim over her. Love and jealousy. Alcohol and rage. Same old, same old, happening over and over throughout history. Curtis was wrong when he said history was just a bunch of stuff not happening now.

Then another thought struck me. I had made her a promise, to reunite her with Geoffrey, but still had no idea how to do that. I looked back to the summer house, beneath the tall trees at the bottom of the lawn. I imagined myself going in there with an armful of bones and presenting them to Ghost-Nancy. But that would hardly work, would it?

"How are we ever going to make this right?" I asked my father.

"You know," he sighed, "from what you've told me, I don't think you can go back there, to the bridge I mean, where you saw Geoffrey, at least not consciously. So maybe all we can do is take these bones away from here, far away from the scene of the crime, get her back home, and then, well maybe Geoffrey can take it from there."

I looked at the small collection of bones. She reminded me of a Guns 'n' Roses song I heard once – all any of us are in the end – dust and bones.

"Come on," said Dad eventually. "We can't sit here all afternoon. If nothing else, there's the washing machine to unload!"

Now, that was a sentence I never thought I'd hear my father utter. It's funny what strikes you as odd. I got gingerly to my feet, legs like two hollowed out cardboard tubes. They wobbled precariously beneath me as we started to carefully pick the bones back up. My shoulder twinged with every movement.

"A hot bath," said Dad, "That's always good for aches and pains. I'll run you one when we get inside."

"You think we should actually stay here tonight?" I looked up at the manor house, standing benignly in the afternoon sunshine, casting its shadow back across the grass as the sun sank a little lower through the trees.

Dad looked too, weighing things up in his mind.

"You know," he said finally, "I could be wrong but I don't feel like the spirits are going to bother us from now on." He looked sadly at the small collection of bones netted in his checked shirt, an incomplete catalogue of someone's short time on this earth. "When everything's out in the open, you have no fight left to fight. It's when you try and cover things up that it all goes wrong."

We walked slowly back across the lawn. Dad. Me. And Nancy-Now.

"Mind you," sighed Dad, "I have absolutely no idea how I'm going to explain all the damage to John

Parker." He started to reel off our list of breakages. "Vase, antique coffee table, bathroom mirror, oh er and don't go into the shed, John, because a bloody great sinkhole has opened up in there..."

"Well, what do you expect when you let the lead singer of Voodoo Mary stay in your crib?" I grinned.

He laughed, gave me a nudge with his elbow and we brought Nancy's remains back into the kitchen for the first time in over one hundred years.

"You fancy going fishing tomorrow?" Dad asked, gently laying the shirt down on the kitchen table and peeling back the edges. "I found some fishing gear in one of those other sheds a couple of days ago. And we've got to do something with the rest of our summer."

The skull of someone long gone but not forgotten stared back at us. It didn't even look that odd any more. But then, that's just how things are with my father.

"Sure Dad," I shrugged. "I mean what could possibly go wrong?"

CHAPTER TWENTY-SEVEN

September

"So, I've got to hand it to you, the locals are not baying for your blood, which must mean the summer wasn't all bad." John Parker was on the phone.

I paused the game we were playing and grabbed my mobile to check for messages.

"I might even go so far as to say you made a new fan or two," added the voice.

"Yeah? Who's that then?" Dad stretched back on the sofa, shouting towards his iPhone on the coffee table. "Not your scary cleaner lady I'll wager?"

"Not exactly. But the gardener did say you weren't as bad as he was expecting. And from him that's high praise."

"Old Parsnip Pete?" Dad sniggered.

"Potato Phil," I corrected him, not that he cared exactly.

"The very same," confirmed John Parker.

"Well, what can I tell you? I'm Craig Cooper, rock legend, enigma, doer of the undoable."

It was Saturday night and I was spending the weekend with my father, that same rock legend, enigma and doer of the undoable, as I did every month.

"Mind you, he did come out with something rather odd," John continued and Dad tensed slightly, ready to punch the speaker button in case it was something I shouldn't overhear. "He said he thought you guys had taken something away from the house." John gave a tight little laugh. "Now, I've been through the place with a fine-toothed comb and apart from the breakages you told me about, I'll be damned if I can find anything else missing." He laughed again but it was a stage-laugh, the kind of laugh they would have taught us to do at acting school no doubt, had Curtis and I continued going. "You want to tell me what he's talking about?"

Dad's eyes flicked to mine then flailed around the room, following the thoughts firing and misfiring in his brain. Eventually he said: "Yeah, we took that old people stink away, that's what we did. We partied hearty, Marty! Yeah!" He made the sign of the horns with his fingers, even though there was no one but me to witness it.

"I'm sure you did, Craig!" John was back on familiar ground, you could tell it from his voice. Sometimes it's comforting – that same old, same old. "Anyway, not to worry. We were down there last weekend, as it turns out. Martina's decided to measure up for new curtains."

"I didn't steal the curtains." Dad threw me a puzzled look. "At least I don't think I did. Adie, did we take the curtains with us? No, I can categorically state that we did not nick your curtains."

"Very funny," John assured him. "No, I'm not sure exactly what's prompted Martina to start redecorating. She's always hated the place. Usually can't get back to London quick enough." (Here Dad threw in a 'yeah, I know that feeling'.) "But, I don't know, suddenly she's talking about spending more time there, holidays and what not."

"You'll have to fill in that ruddy great sink hole first," advised Dad.

"Martina thought we could turn it into a swimming pool."

"Classy." But I'm not sure either of *us* could ever envisage swimming there.

"Yeah, something's definitely fired her imagination about the old place. And of course that means I'm going to have to put my hand in my pocket again to make it all happen. It never stops, does it?"

"You want me to drum up some more business for you, help pay for the pool?" Dad offered. I hoped he was joking but was unable to tell from the eye-roll I got.

"Good God, no." John sounded flustered as if he thought Dad might actually be serious. "No, I'm looking forward to it if I'm honest. Must be my age finally catching up with me. What is it they say, when you're tired of London, you're tired of life?"

"Isn't it when you are tired of *women*, you're tired of life?" Dad quipped back. "That's when you gotta worry."

Now it was my turn to do an eye-roll. It was Samuel Johnson who said that. And it was London, not women. Cara would have known. Maybe my father knew that too but sometimes, like me, he plays it dumb. Something else we have in common.

"Yes well, seems like we'll be spending a little more time at Bridges End from now on, so you *did* breathe some fresh life into the place after all. Thank you for not trashing it, Martina says I have to tell you that."

"Anything for your lovely wife," Dad replied smoothly, already reaching for the game console.

"Okay then." John's voice had the distracted tone of a conversation coming to an end. "But seriously, pool notwithstanding, you know where I am if you need me."

"Sure do." Dad unfroze the action on the screen and the noise started again.

I think I heard John Parker laugh and then the line was dead.

"So I guess we're not telling him *everything* that went down, right?" I checked, glancing momentarily from the TV.

Dad nodded. "You guess right, Adie. You guess right. I think this is going to stay just a family thing for now."

CHAPTER TWENTY-EIGHT

One Year Later

    We flew first class. Well, of course we did. Me and Dad, Mum and Nana Sara, Becky and Lenny. Then came a faceless crew of other people all connected with my father: the best cameraman this side of the Atlantic, said Dad, and a couple of roadies who also doubled as bodyguards along with various other people who milled around on the periphery, making things happen, or stopping things from happening, whatever was required at any given time, and they followed on a few rows further back in economy, their seats determined by their rank and size in the circus that was my father's life, has always been my father's life for as long as I can remember, me – Adie Timothy Cooper, his son and (as far as we all know) his only child, trapeze artist leaping from one precarious platform to another, no visible safety rope, but surviving, always surviving.

    It was greener than I had imagined – that was my first impression of Africa as the plane came into land at Entebbe International Airport. There was a huge lake and palm trees and hills and bushes and the town's name had been carved into a grass bank alongside one runway, in ten-foot high chalk letters, but once we were inside the terminal building we could just as easily have been anywhere else in the world too.

Waiting for us in there was a small, thin, dark-skinned man in a crisp white shirt and black trousers, who had been waiting for some time judging by the flustered damp expression he now wore. (We had been delayed with plane trouble on our stopover in Dubai, which hadn't seemed like a big deal in the first class lounge of Dubai's luxurious airport – at least not to me – but clearly was more of an issue when you were stuck out here, anxiously awaiting your elusive VIP.) The man kept mopping the sweat up into his brow with a navy blue and white checked handkerchief and a look of discomfort on his face as if he was as much a stranger to this land, and this incredible heat, as we were. He apologised over and over for the unprecedented heat-wave that Uganda was experiencing this summer, as if it was somehow his fault.

"We never have it this hot usually," he sighed. "I don't know what is happening to this country!"

And I laughed because it seemed I had heard that somewhere before.

He was our translator, Becky explained, making the introductions, our Mr Fixit for Africa, she said, raising a small bottle of airplane Evian to her lips and taking a short, guarded sip. Olu something or other. The man eyed Nana Sara suspiciously, clearly worried that he had been replaced by some other native between Heathrow and here, looked at my mother – something he couldn't place about her face, part African sure but part something else, turning now to me, but before he could form an opinion he clocked my father, the VIP, the main attraction, loud and very white, head and shoulders and long blond hair above everyone else and his attention was diverted, as always, so that he didn't notice Nana Sara tutting and shaking her head slightly at the crowd which was now starting to form around us, no one sure of who Dad was but sure, just the same, that he was *someone*. The circus had come to Africa. Mr Fixit eventually shooed the curious onlookers away, in a mixture of languages laced with English, and then steered us through Arrivals and onto a baking hot strip of tarmac road that bounced the light up into our eyes so that we had to squint through the intense heat of the afternoon.

    In the taxi to the hotel I craned my neck to peer out of the window, looking for the elephants and the shimmering heat haze of the bush but all around us was the usual hustle and bustle of city living, cars and people and motorbikes, bicycles stacked with sacks of leaves and twigs, all streaming past us or across us, honking horns and shouting. It wasn't the Africa I had imagined: the colourful, almost mystical world that Nana Sara had conjured for me around our kitchen table back in rainy east London. There was no David Attenborough narration for one thing. In its place was a cacophony of discordant noises and voices (that's how I decided I would describe it to Cara when I got back: a cacophony of discordant noises and voices, I liked that) and there was so much dust that it caught at the back of your throat and made your eyes water. Then there were the fumes from all the vehicles, making you tired and slightly woozy, everything moving too fast around you, blurring together to give you a headache. Or maybe I was just a bit too wired to appreciate it properly. I had hardly slept for two days, what with the excitement and everything.

Mum pulled me away from the window, drawing me in for a hug but it was too hot to be close, no air-con in this particular taxi, and our sweaty bodies slid away from one another like repelling magnets. I twisted round in my seat to check that Dad's car was still behind us.

"Adie, sit still for goodness sake," sighed Mum, keeping her voice low so the driver wouldn't hear.

"I've done nothing but sit still for days!" I complained.

"Well, sit still for another ten minutes and then you can jump in the hotel pool. How's that sound?" said Mum.

I flopped restlessly back in the seat, sweat instantly breaking out down my spine, where there was contact with the plastic seat, dampening my Calvin Kleins. I tried to imagine what the pool might be like. Nana Sara rested her head back against the headrest and closed her eyes, a slight smile across her face, the smile of someone who is perfectly at home wherever they are right now.

"So, you never told me," said Mum a couple of minutes later, "who's Nancy?"

I just smiled, and popped the white ear buds back into my ears, a cacophony of a different kind unleashed as Unfathomable Ruination cut loose.

Presently, the hotel loomed into sight before us. In my head I had it all worked out, all the things I wanted to do, in the order I was going to do them. But we had lost a couple of hours in Dubai so now I had to cram an entire afternoon's worth of doing stuff into the remaining part of this first day. Thirty minutes later, I was digging my swimming trunks from the large suitcase half unpacked on the bed.

"And we're having dinner with Dad, right?" I checked, grabbing a towel out of the bathroom, even though most hotels don't like you taking those ones out to the pool area. One of the many advantages of being part of the Craig Cooper entourage: you can pretty much do what you want. Yeah, bathroom towels by the pool: add my name to that long list of hell-raisers.

Mum sighed. I was tiring her out, I knew that, but I was buzzing like I had just drunk ten Red Bulls (which, of course, I hadn't because Mum wouldn't ever let me do such a thing).

"Yes, Adie. Just the four of us." She watched me head for the door. "It's all arranged, don't worry."

I turned and smiled. "I'm not."

'I love you,' she mouthed.

She was probably glad to get rid of me for half an hour. Now she could kick off her shoes and lie down on that big bed with its tight covers and cool iron-flat sheets, home from home.

"Me too," I told her and then I was gone.

I had forgotten the fun of being places with Dad when he was Craig Cooper, Rock Star. He only had to look at a waiter and there was an ice cold glass of Coke on the table, a fresh tray of peanuts. You want to phone Cara? There's a phone topped up with credit. Another pudding? Before you had even decided if you wanted anything the man was there with his pad and pencil. And better still. Want to learn to play Black Jack? Lenny and me went down to the Casino in the hotel basement but Nana Sara came and got me with a disapproving scowl and told me it was time for bed, and I knew better than to tell her she was wrong.

Dad came to say goodnight, catching me out on the balcony in my uncool pyjama bottoms, bare feet, bare chest and still too hot as I looked out at the lights of Africa, twinkling through the blackest night I had ever known.

"It's crazy being here somehow," I said.

"Get some sleep, big day tomorrow," he smiled and I knew he wasn't just talking about the video shoot for Nancy Now And Then, his upcoming single.

"I kept thinking they were gonna find them, you know?" I looked at him, leaning over the hotel balcony, watching the city below, people scuttling and scurrying like cockroaches.

The night air was thick and warm, strangely scented. A patch of sweat formed on my chest where Nancy's gem-stone pendant hung around my neck, glowing warmly with my body heat and the heat of Africa.

"Jesus Adie," said Dad, shaking his long blond hair, "you say anything to anybody and you're probably going to be visiting me in jail for years to come."

"Scouts honour," I told him with a fumble of fingers.

He smiled, still shaking his head at what we had done, and stared back out at the sticky blackness.

The few remaining bones of Nancy-Now, or Nanteza Walusimbi to use her given name, had been smuggled back into the country in a Voodoo Mary amplifier, masquerading as essential musical equipment with all the other various bits and boxes and cases that Dad had insisted on bringing with him. And though Dad's personal carry-on case had been sniffed at by drug dogs, scanned and taken apart item by item at the hands of curious Heathrow officials, the small portable amplifier of bones slipped silently into the cargo hold and off again twenty hours later, Nancy going home. Finally.

We'd done a fair bit of research to try and find out where Nancy may have originally come from and it was a surprise to eventually find that she and my own family were once distant neighbours. Having tracked down the ship that had taken John Wetherby back to the United Kingdom at the turn of the last century, we had come across a name which stood out amongst all the others on the passenger list: Nanteza Walusimbi. We had to assume that this was Nancy-Now. Nana Sara instantly told me this was a Ugandan name suggesting her descendants came from the Ffumbe clan in the east of the country. I remembered the first thing Nancy-Now had said when she saw me: 'you are like me'. Maybe when you scratch any surface, you'll find we all have more 'sames' than differences.

How she had ended up on the dockside in Mombasa, hundreds of miles from her Bugandan village roots is unclear, though I've read that once the railway and the road came to Uganda, it opened up trade links, and one of the commodities being traded was slaves. Somehow, the railway that my great, great, great grandfather had built led Nancy-Now to a port-side slave auction at which John Wetherby just happened to be standing. Did he really believe he was saving her? I wondered what price he had paid for her, buying her life, just to throw it away again in a fit of rage several years later.

Given half the chance, history replays itself over and over. Patterns recur again and again, unless we consciously strive to break the loop of repeat, and that is the hardest thing of all. Just ask my father.

    Africa woke up really early the next morning and as I unglued my eyes I listened to the unfamiliar noises outside my hotel balcony, down on the ground, sensing the heat already rising, listening to a jackhammer as one of the many building projects on this side of town got back underway, voices shouting to one another, cars and motorbikes all zipping around. I reluctantly kicked the one thin bed sheet away from me and lay there, sweating, despite the air-conditioning, tired and slightly muddle-headed but excited and anxious too.

    I met Dad in the foyer after breakfast. He was having a meeting with Becky and Lenny and I patiently waited for them to bring it to a close, mooching round the hotel gift shop for things to take home to Cara and Paul. Eventually Dad came and got me, nodding to Olu, the sweating man with an endless supply of handkerchiefs to mop up his equally endless sweat.

    "Ollie's going to drive us out there," Dad whispered, nodding back to the ever-sweating Olu. "The car's outside."

    Olu held the door open to me as I slid into the back seat. His brow was knitted, slightly confused, no doubt still at a loss as to how he would like pigeon-hole me. Too young to be part of the workforce. Too brown to be Craig Cooper's son. Too white to be anyone else's. I tried not to take offence. If Nancy and Geoffrey's lives had gone the way they'd planned, there would be a whole village of kids just like me living out here. I wasn't so unusual. As Mum always says, we are children of the world, connected in ways that aren't necessarily evident at first glance, but connected just the same.

Dad jumped up into the front seat next to Olu, who he insisted on calling Ollie for some reason, maybe because of his bad hearing.

"Where we go to, Mister Craig Sah?" Olu asked and Dad passed him a post-it note on which he had scrawled the name of a town, several miles north west of here.

We had no way of knowing if this was any closer to Nancy's real home than any other town – it was pretty much down to sticking a pin onto a map of the Buganda region, where we suspected she was originally from, and taking pot luck. This was as good as it was going to get now, seeing as Nancy had vanished after we dug up her bones last summer and neither Dad nor me knew how to summon her back. This strange talent we both shared had not come with an instruction manual and it wasn't the kind of thing you could ask other people. We were both still learning how to use it.

Olu frowned then turned the keys in the ignition and started the engine. Dad twisted round to smile at me. The box containing Nancy-Now's assorted bones sat on the knees of his torn jeans. I looked out of the window again as the streets of the city started to blur past, the cars being the only things out here that seemed to move at speed (and more than compensating for the leisurely pace of everything else). We found ourselves on a fast flat road, full of busses and lorries, cars and taxis, all of us heading out of town. Presently Olu turned on the radio and some gospel type voice crackled out of tinny speakers somewhere behind my head. He turned to my father.

"You like?"

"Sure," Dad smiled, tilting his head back to listen, closing his eyes. "What's life without music?"

The road carried us further west until eventually we were approaching the outskirts of a place called Mpigi.

"Where to Mr Craig, Sah?" asked Olu as we drove into town. Dad shrugged, leaned forward in his seat to look around.

"I don't know exactly."

"You don't know?" Olu sounded worried.

I smiled when I heard the catch in his voice. My father does that to people all the time and doesn't even realise. For once it was nice *not* to be on the receiving end.

"Just keep driving," suggested Dad. "Maybe take us somewhere away from the town."

"You want to go sight-seeing?" Olu checked.

Dad nodded. "Yeah, kind of. Somewhere quiet."

"Okay Sah." Olu drove a little further then turned off the flat main road and headed along a narrower road, bumpy with pot holes. "Not so good road," he announced as we bounced up and down in our seats.

Dad reached for the strap above the window, winding his hand round it to anchor himself inside the car, wedging the box of bones firmly between his legs. Olu kept driving, occasionally looking over to my father as if seeking confirmation that we were still heading the right way, and Dad, not knowing where on earth we were, would nod back and smile.

"What about over there?" Dad pointed to a distant hill bank, dotted with small mushroom-like huts and moments later Olu obligingly yanked the wheel onto a dirt track, leaving the tarmac behind altogether.

"Are you certain Mister Craig, Sah, this is where you want to go?" asked Olu taking his eyes off the red dirt road just long enough for me to grip the back of my father's seat with a rising sense of panic.

The car bounced up and down over the packed earth, seemingly driving itself.

"Yeah, yeah, just keep driving," said Dad, his free hand zipping the green pendant up and down the loop of black leather around his neck. "I'll tell you when to stop."

I felt for my own pendant nestling in the slight hollow of my chest bone, keeping Nancy close. We drove on, the gospel choir being replaced with a woman's soft voice singing some kind of pop song. A little later, we stopped at an isolated shack at the side of the road. It sold cold drinks and chewing gum and small packets of biscuits. More tinny music filtered out into the hot space around it. The owner of the shack popped the tops on a couple of bottles of Fanta and passed them to my father and me. He looked at Olu, questioning, but no answer was spoken out loud.

"Four-hundred-and-eighty days clean and sober," announced Dad clinking his bottle with mine before he raised it to his lips.

"That's great Dad." I drank thirstily.

"We'll have a party when I get to five-hundred, right?" he winked.

We drained our bottles and then got back into the car and started driving again. Red road. Green bushes. Banana trees with thick shiny leaves. A village. Gone again. A stretch of tarmac that started for no reason and stopped just as abruptly, the red dirt road beginning over again. The noise of a hundred crickets and other insects scratching out their calls to each other like static. Clouds sitting over the hilltops in the distance, heavy with impending rain. The heat-wave was going to break any day now, promised Olu.

"Here! Stop."

Olu slammed on the brakes, throwing us forward in our seats.

Dad twisted round to look at me, eyebrows raised in a question. I shrugged. We appeared to be in the middle of a scrubby bit of land, which seemed just the same as the last few miles, except for a few houses in the far distance partially hidden by a broken down wall. I looked around. Clumps of emerald-green plants grew thickly out of the flat, dusty orange earth, all resting under a pale blue and endless sky. These were the colours Nana Sara always spoke about.

"Here, Adie, I think, yeah?"

We got out of the car. The heat was like you get from opening the oven door and looking inside. I could feel it pressing on my skin, an entity in its own right. Olu got out of the car and wiped the handkerchief across his face once more, then lit himself a cigarette and looked to the clouds sitting on top of the far hill, nudging the horizon. Once the rain came this road would be pretty much impassable. Dad nodded to me and we started to walk away from the car so that he wouldn't see us.

"Mister Craig, Sah!" shouted Olu, concerned that he was losing his VIP, his precious cargo, his wage packet; concerned what Becky would say or do if he lost this very important man, Mr Craig Sah, whoever the hell that was.

"Yeah, yeah." Dad waved his hand at him. "Back in a minute, I promise."

We walked just a little way from the vehicle, disappearing behind another banana tree before Dad stopped and looked furtively around him. I pressed record on my phone, scanning the panorama.

"Good thinking." Dad set the box down on the flame-coloured ground. "We can use a bit of your footage in our video, if it's any good."

He opened the top to gently lift out the skull of someone we had both known a long, long time ago. He glanced back one more time to check that Olu wasn't coming over too. Then, crouching down, he took out the various bits of bone and laid them all down on the rough African earth. The heat bounced up off the ground to meet us.

"Shouldn't we say something?" I whispered, kneeling beside him.

"Like what?"

"I don't know."

Dad rearranged the bones in the red, African dirt. The static rose up between us. I swatted away a mosquito tickling the back of my neck and we crouched there, looking around, feeling the hot dry soil under our fingertips.

"Hey Dad, do you ever wonder whether Grandpa has this thing too?"

He looked at me. A bead of sweat travelled down his forehead and he squinted as it rolled into one eye. "My father? My father talk to ghosts?" He blinked, stared at the ground, at the little pile of bones, brushed away a few small stones as if making it nice for Nancy-Now. "No, Ade, I never really thought about it before."

"Maybe you should ask him," I shrugged and he gave me a half-hearted 'maybe'.

Black ants scampered around us, now exploring the strange bones that had been placed in their world. I thought I heard a roll of thunder, far away, a warning of things to come.

"Rain's coming," noted Dad, sounding like a local.

I looked again at the small skull, hollowed out eye sockets staring blankly across the orange-dust floor. "I definitely feel like we should say something, but there's nothing to say, is there?" I turned to my dad.

When it comes to condensing an entire life into a few short words, whatever you say is going to be inadequate.

"Goodbye Nancy," Dad whispered, smiling. "Thank you for everything. It was good to know you."

He stood up.

"I hope you find Geoffrey." I stood up too. "I won't ever forget you. You did more than you realise."

The sweat trickled down my back, squeezing out from my armpits. The rain clouds seemed to be coming down the mountain towards us, the air thick and heavy with expectant thunder. Back beyond the car, where Olu stood smoking, a heat haze shimmered, like a mirage, stretching off into the far distance, blurring the lines of the grass and the trees, the sky and the clouds, so that you couldn't be sure where the earth ended and the sky began. I looked into its filmy haze. Africa. Finally.

"Come on." Dad clapped a hand across my shoulder, the heat of it almost unbearable as the time approached noon but I was reluctant to shrug it off. "We've still got a music video to shoot, remember?"

And with that we walked slowly back to the car, Olu throwing down his cigarette and jumping excitedly back inside, bright white smile against dark brown skin, his relief plain to see, thankful that all was well again.

Other titles in this series:

A Leather Jacket
No Man's Land

Discover more at mynextbigbook.com

Printed in Great Britain
by Amazon